W9-AVG-265

AMERICAN PROBLEMS

AMERICAN PROBLEMS

FROM THE POINT OF VIEW
OF A PSYCHOLOGIST

BY

HUGO MÜNSTERBERG

Essay Index Reprint Series

BOOKS FOR LIBRARIES PRESS
FREEPORT, NEW YORK

First Published 1910
Reprinted 1969

STANDARD BOOK NUMBER:
8369-1098-2

LIBRARY OF CONGRESS CATALOG CARD NUMBER:
75-84328

PRINTED IN THE UNITED STATES OF AMERICA

TO

FRIEDRICH SCHMIDT

A MASTER-BUILDER

OF

GERMAN-AMERICAN FRIENDSHIP

CONTENTS

PREFACE

American problems have tempted me to enter into public discussion ever since I became a guest in this hospitable land. But naturally the point of view has shifted somewhat. The first instinctive impulse was to compare the new impressions with those to which I was accustomed, and thus to measure American institutions by German standards. It was the newcomer's point of view from which I wrote my " American Traits." But while the aim of that book was to bring German ideals nearer to the American public, my deepest interest in American problems soon led to the opposite effort. I tried to show American work and American ideals to the Germans. This time my purpose was to give a systematic view of the American people. The book was written in German and later was translated into English under the title "The Americans."

But in the meantime I have become one of them. While I have remained a German citizen, I naturally have accepted the American point of view more and more. Impressions which at first struck me as strange slowly have become a matter of course. My interest in American problems has not decreased on this account, but the angle from which I see them has become a new one. It is no longer the national difference but more my professional lifework which has influenced my attitude toward the public questions. Not as a German but as a psychologist I have begun to take sides as to problems which stir the nation.

In this spirit the following essays are written. Of course this psychological interest determines somewhat the selection of the subjects which I discuss. Problems like those of scholarship and education, of temperance and customs, of superstition and nervousness, stand nearer to the psychologist than those of trusts and tax legislation. Some may even think that this tends to exclude the real problems before the American mind and to give attention only to the by-problems. And yet in certain respects may not the less important problems be the most important ones?

All these essays have appeared in magazines, in The Atlantic Monthly, in McClure's Magazine, in the Metropolitan Magazine and so on, and I am obliged to them for the right to a new appearance. Practically every one of these papers has been discussed with unusual energy throughout the newspapers of the country. May a part of this generous interest be maintained for this little book. I have revised the papers to a slight degree but only in the case of the essay on prohibition have I hoped to secure a better understanding by adding a lengthy epilogue.

HUGO MÜNSTERBERG.

Harvard University.
March 1910.

I

THE FEAR OF NERVES

THE FEAR OF NERVES

BEFORE and since Molière's immortal comedy, he who fancies himself to be the victim of a disease and suffers from imaginary symptoms has always been the target of merry jests. But in modern times we see the more serious aspect of the case. On the one side, we know that to imagine symptoms of disease can be itself the expression of an abnormal state. And, above all, on the other side, to think oneself into the rôle of the patient can be the starting-point for serious disturbances. By a kind of auto-suggestion, the healthy man becomes really ill if he fixates his mind on the symptoms which he believes he feels. This curious and by no means harmless state may befall not only individuals, but whole nations, whole generations. Society to-day, and especially the social body of America, imagines itself to be the pitiable victim of a miserable disease: general nervousness.

Indeed, it is a dogma of our generation, not that this or that man suffers from neurasthenia or other nervous diseases, but that our whole nervous make-up has become worse; that nervous troubles are on the increase; that our entire social life has become neurasthenic, and that we must do our utmost to protect our nerve energies against the tiredness and exhaustion which have become the habitual fate.   Our time knows the symptoms, knows the conditions, knows the remedies of this national disease, and all fits together so nicely that the theory seems secure. No one has a right to doubt the facts any longer.   All that remains is to take care that we get a strong dose of the remedies.   All parties concerned seem so perfectly satisfied with this vista of social psychology that it might seem easiest not to scrutinize the case, and not to play the physician who unkindly insists that he wants not only to hear the complaints of the patient, but also to feel his pulse and measure his temperature and examine his lungs and heart.   Yet here, too, the case may be one in which the imagined disease will easily become the source of real organic trouble.   If our time goes on thinking itself abnormally nervous, it may indeed finally become ill; and there are not a few indications that care is necessary. Thus, a little scrutiny may be useful after all.

The symptoms of the imagined disease are told us everywhere.   Most easily visible is the general hurry and restlessness.   Whether we see the individual rush to his business or devour his lunch, see the overflow of useless movements from the chewing of gum to the ceaseless motion of the rocking chair, or watch the hustling and pushing of the public life, the hasty passing from one interest to another, everything suggests a nervous condition of society.   There is a social unrest which indicates an inner nervous irritation. But nervousness shows itself not only in jerky, twitchy movements but, at the same time, in a quick exhaustion of the nervous energy. We need vacations and excursions, the rest of country life and frequent changes more than any previous generation. Our nerve-energy is so run down that we can get refreshment only by tickling amusements. After the day's work, who still has the mental force to see a tragedy on the stage? The nerves of our time demand musical comedies. Who still has the inner concentration to read books? In the last twenty-five years the number of our book-stores has melted down to less than a third, in spite of the increase of the population. We are too nervous to read books. Our nerves can stand only the light short-cut magazine articles. This story of nervous restlessness and nervous fatigue comes to its greatest expression in the rapid increase of nervous diseases. Two-thirds of our acquaintances have neurasthenia, and nervous prostration is the fashion for men and women alike. Psychasthenic and hysteric symptoms abound, and the waiting-rooms of the nerve specialists are crowded.

But there is no need to point to the symptoms, as they can easily be foreseen as the necessary and natural consequences of the nerve-racking conditions under which we are bound to live. How often have we heard that our age is that of electricity. Every new invention and every discovery has hastened the whole rhythm of our life. The *adagio* of our forefathers has become a *prestissimo* which

must keep us breathless.   And with the haste has come
the noise.   The metropolitan who has to think while the
telephone rings and the elevated roars and the typewriter
hammers must be a wreck before he is through with his
work.   Yet, endlessly worse is the inner tension of the life,
the multiplicity of our engagements, the pressure of the
responsibilities, and above all the sharpness of the competition.   It may be that the newspapers are especially responsible.   They have enlarged our sphere, so that every
day heaps upon us a thousand exciting reports from all
over the globe.   There is no calling and no profession
which does not feel the new, unsafe tension.   Truly, it is
not only the broker at the stock exchange whose emotions
become over-strained.   The conditions of the market-place
have become such that everybody is over-burdened and has
much more to do than his grandfather ever thought of doing.   We are forced to automobile through life, and the
fugitive impressions of the world through which we are
racing must bewilder us and make us dizzy.   There is
no longer any repose or any relief.   Our poor nerves are
maltreated from morning to night, from childhood to old
age.   The nervousness of our time comes with the necessity of a natural effect.

The only thing to be hoped for is at least to find some
good remedies, and if we cannot effect a cure, as the case
seems desperate, we may bring some passing alleviation.
The most immediate help is, of course, the medical.   The
public does not wait for the physician, but supplies itself
with all the nervina from aspirine to the glycerophos-

phates. But the official drugs cannot suffice for the growing demand for nerve cures. Mental healing and faith cures of all types, Christian Science and church clinics have been superadded. Every day creates new schemes for smoothing the irritated and the exhausted nervous system. Moreover, we try to eliminate at least the unnecessary scratching of our poor nerves. The wave of abstinence legislation has swept over the country. Alcohol surely is poison for weak nerves, but coffee is no better, and tobacco ruins them in another way. The crusade against artificial stimuli is controlled by an instinctive desire to save our wrecked nervous substance. The movement from the city to the country, to the seashore and mountains, aims towards the same goal. We instinctively feel that fresh air and sunshine may bring back to us what we have lost among skyscrapers and smoky chimneys. And best of all, at last the whole nation has learned the blessing of physical exercise. However our daily life may cripple our nerves and our whole organism, everyone nowadays understands that at least half an hour a day must be devoted to physical exercise in order to restore the machinery. Whether we swing the dumb-bells or the golf stick, whether we bicycle or play ball or run, the nerve cure of regular bodily activity has at last been accepted by young and old, by rich and poor, by men and women, by the higher and the lower classes. If we had not this everpresent remedy, the nervousness of the time would be intolerable.

This story of the symptoms, the causes, and the remedies has become the stock equipment of our social neurology, and he who dares to doubt knows that he finds no neutral hearers. Nevertheless, I do not hesitate to claim that this story is imaginative from beginning to end. And if the prejudices are allowed to spread as in recent years, the belief in this self-made disease may indeed become a serious handicap. It is an illusion that our time is more nervous than earlier periods; it is an illusion that the material and social conditions under which we live are favorable to nervous diseases; it is an illusion that the highly-praised remedies would really serve their purpose if the disease existed.

To begin with the end, must it really be kept a secret that the dogma of the physical exercise is typical of this whole fabric of imagination? If once we liberate ourselves from the hygienic cant with which our time is overflooded we must recognize the comic aspect of the situation. Millions of people are running wildly to catch a ball, lifting weights in fullest perspiration, trotting with gasping breath, and doing a hundred other useless tricks simply because a meaningless fashion has cruelly thrown them into such a habit. Of course it seems as if the opposite may quickly be proved. Ask the man on the street whether he would not feel miserably if he gave up his daily exercise, and he will tell you from the bottom of his heart that he cannot live without it. He is right; and yet he is no more right than the morphinist who feels in despair and suffers if he cannot have his injection; no more right than the habitual drinker who would not find sleep at night if he did not have his three mugs of beer after supper, or the

other type who would have no appetite if he had no cocktail before the soup.   Certainly our whole central nervous system adjusts itself rapidly to new forms of stimulation, and is in a poor state if the habitual excitement is
taken away.   A craving sets in which must be satisfied.
We do not know much about the mechanism, but the facts
cannot be doubted.   The brain of the smoker really has
to suffer if the accustomed daily stimulus is omitted.   Is
it the right conclusion that for this reason smoking is
necessary for the welfare of the human organism?

Regular physical exercise of the artificial kind is a habit
which, just like the moderate use of light alcoholic beverages, has certain advantages, but which must also be held
within the closest limits, unless the disadvantages are to
be greater.   Certainly it is no less artificially introduced
into our social life, and in this case, too, it is just as wise
not to allow it to become a habit.   To wander through the
country on a fine day is a beautiful inspiration, and healthful for everyone; to need the walk with mechanical regu-
larity is the product of a bad training, and to become the
slave of Swedish gymnastic apparatus is no better than
slavery to cigars.   Of course, for certain purposes, it is
desirable to develop the muscular forces of the body; then
the physical exercise becomes labor.   That is an entirely
different thing.   For certain others, especially educational
purposes, it is most desirable to have sport and competi-
tive athletics; then the physical effort becomes pleasure
and play.   But as mere exercise and restoration, it is need-
less in moderation and harmful in strong doses, and the

necessity only results from the long training in it.   For a long time the pedagogue even believed that muscular effort was the best recreation after the intellectual work of the school child.   Nowadays we know that the opposite is true.   Physical exercise demands the energies of the same brain which learns the school lesson and the fatigued brain becomes still more strained if its energies are tapped for a new activity.   There is only one source of restitution of used-up brain energy, and that is rest and sleep, together with fresh air and good nourishment.   If the craving for physical exercise is not intentionally injected into the body by habitual indulgence in this useless stimulation, the normal personality can do just as good work and remain just as well without such strained effort.   Moreover, he enjoys the moderate, occasional use of exercise far more.

No less doubtful in their final effectiveness are the other popular remedies for the nerve troubles of our time.   It is certainly no gain that headache powders and the sleeping drugs belong to the equipment of every fashionable woman, and that they are sold over the counter of the soda-fountain.   A passing discomfort is too often removed at the expense of really healthy nerves.   Still worse is the psychotherapy of dilettanti.   It seems to me one of the best indications of the splendid nervous constitution of the nation that it has passed with so little serious harm through the millionfold attacks on its nervous system which the amateurish psychotherapists of every denomination have directed against it.   Most of that which the faith healers and mind curists and Christian Scientists and their kin are performing is very well meant and faithfully carried out, but splendidly arranged to create at least mild hysteria in weak nervous systems. Enviable is the race which shows sufficient nerve-strength to pass through it without real damage.

Yet the illusions are still queerer when our conditions of life are blamed as necessary causes of nervous exhaustion. Is not the nearest aim of our much-advertised technical civilization to save our nerve-energy? It is true that the electric current runs rapidly through the wire, but do we not let it run, so that we may remain quietly seated instead of running ourselves? The technical mechanism of our life has become more complex just for the sake of making our life itself simpler. The telephone at our desk and the elevator in our hall save us trouble. Where can we find more rest than on an express train? It is true its engine runs faster than that of the slow train, but that does not mean that we feel in a greater hurry when we are comfortably seated in the parlor car of the Limited. Our poor forefathers had to go through much nerve-irritation, but our life is smooth. How their visual brain centers must have suffered from their flickering light and from the astigmatism of lenses in the eye! We have mild, steady light, and the oculist corrects our lenses. Our triumphing natural science, with all its marvelous inventions, with its progress of hygiene and pathology, has primarily removed the friction. Instead of a rough, rocky road, we move along on a smooth, asphalt street, over which there is really no difficulty in proceeding.

Of course it is true that the social life has become more manifold and the outer tension has become stronger; but it is entirely misleading to believe that that is in itself a greater strain on the nervous system. The scientific psychologist brings no clearer conviction from his laboratory study of mental life than that of the relativity of mental states. Our attention, our feeling, our interest, our excitement never depend upon the mere amount of the stimulus. The same amount may make a strong impression at one time, at another a faint one, again under other conditions no impression at all. Everything depends upon its relation to the background. If three voices are shouting, the noise becomes noticeably stronger when a fourth is added, but if thirty are heard, one more or even five more will not be heard: ten more would have to join to make a perceptible difference. And if three hundred produce a noise, fifty more will not add anything: now a hundred must be brought in to secure the slightest growth in intensity of the sound. The shouting of the hundred men when they fall in with three hundred makes no more impression than one man when he joins only three others. This law prevails universally. The conditions for a feeling of difference, and therefore for an emotional excitement, are always relative. Two street boys who quarrel about a cent are no less enraged than two captains of industry who quarrel about a million. It is absurd to measure the effect of our surroundings on our brain by the mere mass and size and strength of the attacking stimulus. The proportion alone is decisive. What may be the source of strongest emotion in the colorless village life may be a hardly noticeable, mild variation for the globe-trotter, which leaves scarcely a trace in his mind.

No less important is another psychological fact: the mental adaptation which slowly levels down even the strongest impression. The miller does not hear the noise of the mill. No one of us feels the touch of his clothes. In the same way we have become insensitive by adaptation to our tumultuous surroundings. When we return from the mountain woods, we hear the roaring of the city for a day or two, and then it sinks below our consciousness and no longer harms our well-adapted nerves.

Moreover, while our modern life has become more manifold, its emotional strain is rather less severe than that of the past. Our life is less sentimental and more realistic and businesslike. No longer do we write the letters full of feeling which our grandparents wrote: we of to-day dictate notes. We do not keep emotional diaries: instead, we subscribe to the clipping bureau. Above all, our public life and our welfare is less threatened by dangers and sudden changes — the chief source of nervous shocks. Not only the meteorologist of the weather bureau tells us a long time beforehand when the thunder-storm or the hailstorm is to come; our social life and our politics in this age of the cable are served by their weather bureaus, too. Excitement and public fear have been tuned down. Our growing tolerance works in the same manner. Conflicts are less embittered. On the whole we enjoy our disagreements and make pleasant after-dinner speeches out of them, and applaud the good stories of our opponent. This is no age for being especially nervous.

Of course it cannot be overlooked that such inner changes never move in one direction only. They may remove certain evils and open the sources of others. A simple yes or no does not answer such complex questions. For instance, we pointed out that a reason for the nervousness of earlier generations was emotionalism and sentimentality, and that this has yielded to a cooler mutual relation of men. In the light of modern psychopathology we begin to understand that this may, nevertheless, be a condition for nervousness of a very different kind. Recent years have shown that many of the hysteric and psychasthenic disturbances are simply the result of a suppressed memory of disagreeable experiences. An unpleasurable event which failed to find its natural expression becomes in a way strangulated in the mind and begins to work mischief there in the brain centers, even without conscious knowledge of the person. Now it is evident that sentimentality brings with it a mutual confidence and intimacy in which everyone finds many more opportunities of expressing the feelings of his mind, and thus disburdening his inner life from such mischievous intrusions. The businesslike soberness of our modern times has taken away this chance for confession; and many a nervous system may be wrecked, where a confessional might have saved it. This shows how the ideal mental state cannot be prescribed by a simple psychological formula, but at least so much ought to be clear to the social psychologist, that neither our nervous system nor the surroundings of our life should be blamed for our tiredness and restlessness. ―

But there is no need of going on showing the illusory ideas as to the causes of our general nervousness. We can take a straighter road and insist that this nervousness itself is an illusion. Of course, nervous diseases are plentiful; and whatever medical science can do to relieve them, and whatever hygiene can do to prevent them, must be done most earnestly and insistently. The recent development of scientific psychotherapy promises much for the alleviation of this human burden. But the more ready recognition of nervous diseases does not justify the claim that nervousness has rapidly increased, and that it is the signature of our time. And what is more important, in no way does it justify the nervousness over nervousness which has been spread by this uncritical acceptance of the illusory claim. It is arbitrary, for instance, to see in the rush and hurry a sign of nervousness. It is practically a sign of lack of co-ordination, a certain remainder of untrained impulsiveness and disconnectedness of movements which, on the whole, begins to disappear, or at least to be pushed westward. The jerky movements, the chewing and rocking and putting the feet on the table will soon be overcome, just as the spitting has nearly disappeared from the Eastern cities. On the contrary, the Americans strike the observant foreigner as rather too patient. They are ready to tolerate delays and to wait quietly where the European would have become irritated, and they waste time wherever there is the least opportunity as only a very rich nation can

afford to do.   They begin their youth by wasting at least
two years in school, reaching at nineteen a point which
every intelligent being can certainly reach — by seventeen.
After such thorough training in time-wasting, they per-
sistently carry on the method.   It is an illusion to believe
that they change it and become time-saving simply because
in traveling they jump up from their seats and rush to the
end of the car ten minutes before their train reaches the
station.

Of course the reports of the hospitals and of the doctors
seem to speak with figures.   But may it not be with our
psychasthenias and neurasthenias as it was when appendicitis became fashionable?   The statistical reports of a
certain European army showed that in ten years the
number of appendicitis cases became four times larger,
but a further scrutiny of the statistics demonstrated that
exactly in the same percentage in which this favorite disease was growing, all which had been classed as general intestinal troubles happily decreased.   In short, it
was evident that the spreading of the dreaded ailment
was an illusion.   It had only found a new name.   Now
it certainly is well that we have all the new names for
the nervous disturbances and that we understand their
character better to-day, but indeed a danger arises if this
knowledge is turned into a discouragement, into an exaggerated attentiveness to states which an earlier period
ignored or simply handled as variations of temperament
and mood and imagination and will.   Yes, the history of
medicine points rather clearly to the opposite fact that

nervous diseases have become less general, compared perhaps with medieval times. At least our time is spared the nervous epidemics of former centuries.

Least of all ought we to measure the good or poor states of our national nerves by the complaints of tiredness. It is true there are persons who demand from their nerves more than hygienic life would allow because they are too little provided with the healthy feeling of fatigue which nature has arranged as a warning sign for the exhaustion of the nervous system. But incomparably larger is the number of those who have trained themselves to feel fatigued long before any exhaustion is threatening. It is a weakness of will and attention which causes the deceitful impression of nervous exhaustion, which is really nothing but a poor habit. Imitation plays a big rôle in it; continuous indulgence a greater. The longing for rest and for interruption of regular work can become just as much a craving and vicious custom as the longing for stimulants. And just as every new artificial stimulation reënforces the desire, every new yielding to such pseudo-tiredness makes work more and more uncomfortable.

Here we have finally reached a true evil which cannot be brushed aside as an illusion; yes, an evil which is too often responsible for that national fancy of general nervousness. That from which the people really suffer, and perhaps suffer more than any other nation, more than any other time, is the weakness of attention. To be sure attention is a function of the brain, and therefore ultimately is an act of our nervous system. But its weakness and lack of development is not a nervous disease; it is a bad habit of the nerves, but not nervousness. It is a wrong of the mind, but not a mental disease. And because this true evil is spreading in a most dangerous way it is important to recognize it and to warn against any misunderstanding, as if the symptoms which result from it were symptoms which demand the physician. The more the confusion between lack of attention and nervous weakness is favored, the greater are the chances that we shall coddle the nerves more and more, and in that way create nervous diseases without curing the fundamental wrong.

The foreigner who studies the American character will always be deeply impressed by the wonderful striving for self-assertion, self-perfection, and self-realization, which gives meaning and significance to this greatest democracy of the world. But there is one trait which he instinctively perceives, in spite of all his enthusiasm in the strength and glory of the New World. He cannot help feeling the lack of accuracy and thoroughness, the superficiality, the go-as-you-please character of the work; and this ultimately always means the lack of voluntary attention. The small respect for the expert in every field, the condescending smile for the dry theory, belong together with the carelessness with which the girls spell and the boys calculate. Every feature of our social life shows an unwillingness to concentrate attention. Only that which can be followed without effort is welcome. The serious drama is deserted, and the vaudeville houses are crowded; the serious editorials of the newspapers disappear, and the racy style wins success; the yellow-press tone colors larger and larger parts of politics, and even of court and church. And yet what else is the meaning of it but the victory of involuntary attention and the defeat of voluntary attention?

Human nature is indeed so arranged that the attention at first follows in an involuntary way all that is shining, loud, sensational and surprising. The real development of mankind lies in the growth of the voluntary attention; which is not passively attracted, but which turns actively to that which is important and significant and valuable in itself. No one is born with such a power. It has to be trained and educated. Yes, perhaps the deepest meaning of education is to secure this mental energy which emancipates itself from haphazard stimulations of the world and firmly holds that which conforms to our purposes and ideals. This great function of education is too much neglected. As a reaction against a rigid, empty, mechanical instruction, there swept over the country a wave of electivism which was meant to bring the blessings of freedom, but which did bring primarily a destruction of self-discipline. It is not difficult to foresee that much of this work must be undone. If kindergarten methods are allowed to penetrate where self-discipline of attention should be learned, the future citizen has lost his chance.

Whoever is allowed always to follow the path of least

resistance will soon find any work drudgery and any effort tiring and a torture to his nerves. A child who
never has received an order, but who at six years of age
has been only begged and persuaded, will never be his
own master at twenty-six. Self-control demands a long
preparation, and lack of self-control is only another name
for many of those symptoms which the outsider calls
nervousness. There is no work in the world most of
which is not drudgery and an irritation to the nerves for
one who, in his time of education, forgot to learn the
joy of doing his duty. I read this morning in a great
newspaper: "There are few more trying and nerve-
wrecking tasks than that of beating eggs by hand; to
keep the hand moving at the right speed requires the concentration of much nerve-force." I have never tried it
myself, and therefore cannot compare this "nerve-wrecking task" with some other exhausting demands which
this cruel age of ours requires from our nervous system;
but I feel sure that they are mostly of similar character.
And while I see with delight from the same article that
this particular scourge of mankind has lost its terror,
since a machine has been invented with a paddle that
works automatically to beat eggs, I am certain that in
the meantime this type of mind has discovered a score
of other nerve-wrecking tasks. Seriously, the more we
spoil our attention and cultivate in ourselves the passive
attitude which is driven hither and thither by every
changing event, the more we must become frightened by
the real work of the world which does not allow us to

shift. The school-teacher is more important for curing the nervousness of our time than the physician.

But one other important point must not be overlooked if we try to understand why the surface view of our social life gives such an impression of nervous restlessness. It is the predominance of the feminine mind in the shaping of national society. The other day I heard a solemn speech by an old gentleman who declared once more that the chief difference between our age and the past is the technical discoveries. Some days later I gained much deeper wisdom from the lips of a little boy. I was visiting a large new school in Buffalo. The principal brought me into a history class where the children had just been learning about the old Romans and their family organization. The first question which the young woman teacher asked in our presence was the momentous one: " What do you think is the greatest difference between the life of the old Romans and our modern American life? " She pointed to a little boy who arose and said: " With the old Romans the father was the head of the family." The whole situation was illuminated in a marvelous way.

Yes, in our age the woman is the head of the family, and the woman is the head of our social life; is the head of our art and literature; is the head of our social reforms and our public movements; is the head of our intellectual culture and of our moral development. Who can deny that it has brought to the nation an abundance of help and of charm? It has kept alive the nobler interests when the men's energies were absorbed by the rough pioneer work of the land. But for this very reason, it was unavoidable that public life should have accepted many characteristic features which belong essentially to the female mind. And there is none more typical than the shifting of attention. The feminine mind certainly has an inferior power of inhibition and therefore less energy of concentration. If we characterize it in this way, it sounds as if it were a defect, but shadow and light lie near together. The woman does not inhibit; she lives less in abstractions and, ultimately, that means that she sees things and persons in their wholeness, where men see only one-sided aspects. In short, this peculiarity of the feminine mind has its great advantages. It will do much more justice to a personality, because all aspects are considered, the attention moving from one to another. It is the ideal mental condition for work which demands plenty of small detail, where the attention has to go from one thing to another without any long focusing at a particular point. Here centers the remarkable talent of the woman for the care of the home; here lies her wonderful influence for harmony and beauty, for the conservation of traditions, and for the emotional life.

But all these talents and traits of the woman's mind must produce very different effects when her sphere of activity becomes unrestricted. That which gives charming lightness to the female activity in the narrower sphere easily becomes a flippant superficiality and a nervous restlessness in the wider realm. The predominance of women with quickly moving attention gives to the American life a general aspect of haste and nervousness, where every movement is quickly taken up and quickly forgotten, where fads and fancies are alternating with undignified rapidity, and where public discussions too often remain superficial and controlled by feeling.

Hence, in order to cure the so-called nervousness of our time, the remedies ought to be adapted to these true evils. The dumb-bells and bromides are not enough. On the one side we need more training in self-discipline, in continuous effort, in voluntary attention, and in thoroughness; and on the other, more willingness of the men to share with the women the control of our cultural life, and to bring to it steadiness and persistence. This self-discipline will also eliminate many nuisances which, from a medical point of view, really interfere with nervous health. For instance, the whole radicalism of the prohibition movement would not be necessary if there were more training for self-control. To prohibit always means only the removal of the temptation, but what is endlessly more important is to remain temperate in the midst of a world of temptation. The rapid growth of divorce, the silly chase for luxury, the rivalry in ostentation and in the gratification of personal desires in a hundred forms cannot be cured if only one or another temptation is taken out of sight. The improvement must come from within. The fault is in ourselves, in our prejudices, in our training, in our habits, and in our fanciful fear of nervousness.

II

THE CHOICE OF A VOCATION

II

THE CHOICE OF A VOCATION

IN those colleges where the choice of a course is left to the student, it is always interesting to inquire into the motives that guide the preference. Of the hundreds who flock to a course in history, or economics, or chemistry, or literature, certainly there are many who know that they have chosen the course that they need and the one that will be most profitable for their inner development. But there are others, and those others are far too many. Some students select a course because their friends are taking it, others because they have heard that it is a " soft snap." Sometimes a course is chosen because the lecturer is well known for his witty remarks, sometimes because the lecture hour conflicts least with the training for athletics, and again because the lecture room is conveniently located downstairs or because the books needed for the course are small enough to be carried in the pocket.

On the whole, this situation also pictures the methods by which the American youth chooses his life work. The overwhelming majority must enter upon a bread-winning life when the graded school has been passed. Here also a large number certainly have an aim and a goal, and with firm step they enter the chosen path. But a discouraging number of boys and girls are drifting here and there from haphazard motives and most trivial causes. The hasty advice of an incompetent friend, a chance advertisement, a superficial liking for some surface features of a calling without any knowledge of its real duties, a vague illusory idea as to the great financial rewards of a line of work, push a boy in this or that direction. As he has not been trained for any definite thing, and has neither a conscious preference nor sufficient knowledge of the social world with its openings and its opportunities, he is glad to slip in anywhere.

All this repeats itself, not very differently though on a somewhat higher level, with that smaller part of the population that has passed through the high schools. To be sure, those four additional years have given to many a boy a wholesome opportunity to find himself and to discover his aptitudes and interests. But, if we watch the further development, we witness the depressing sight of the same haphazard selection of a practical career, the same ignorance, the same valuation of petty circumstances, the same drifting. The most important step in life is often taken with hardly more deliberation than many of those boys would use in selecting a new suit of clothes.

The student who recklessly chooses his lecture course in college may lose the highest gain, but the result will not be serious harm. Every course is planned so as to give him something of value. But an unsuitable life course may result in real harm — yes, in failure and wreck. Surely the divorce mills of the country have enough to do; but the cases in which a man is divorced from his profession, or at least ought to be divorced from it if his life is not to be misery to him, are even more numerous. Yet, the cases of failure are not the only ones that count against the present system. From the national point of view, the absurd wastefulness condemns this reckless scheme no less. The boy who drives a butcher's cart, then becomes call boy in a hotel, afterward goes to work in a factory, and a few weeks later tries the next chance job that offers itself, loses the great advantage of systematic training for a definite task.

No one can deny that this careless shifting and unprepared entrance upon a life career is dangerously favored by certain conditions of American life. Politics and the whole social structure of the country have always encouraged the view that everybody is fit for everything. The traditional disrespect for the expert, the old-fashioned spoils system, the tendency of democracy to put the technical government of towns into the hands of untrained men, have too long reinforced the impression that nothing but the possession of intelligence and energy are necessary to fill any place. The absence of social barriers and the predominance of the money influence, the lack of discipline and authority in the education of the youth, and, perhaps strongest of all, the natural wealth of the nation, work in the same direction. The country could afford the limitless waste of human energies, just as it

felt justified in wasting the timber resources of the forest.
*. But in recent years all this has changed.   The more
complex conditions of modern life, the progress of science
and economics, of sanitation and education, have gradually taught the country a new respect for the services of
the expert; the devastating spoils system has had to
yield, and the national conscience has forcefully awaked
in its protest against the waste of the national resources.
This new spirit has at last started a growing conviction
among thinking people that something must be done for
the youth who seeks a vocation.

To many the most natural way would seem to be in a
reorganization of the schools.   Indeed, it has often been
proposed to give to the child a greater chance for specialization, even in the lower schools.   In this way the school
might develop little specialists who would be better prepared than others for certain lines of work, and who would
be more successful through such early training.   Moreover, the school would have opportunity to adjust such
early specialization to the gifts and predominant interests
of the individual boy or girl.   But a more thorough study
of the functions of the public school sounds a decided
warning against this tendency.   Dangers lurk there on all
sides.   The safety of the nation demands a real common ground for the whole population, a common education in the fundamentals of the national life.   The more
years the youth of the country can devote to a general
education, the more wholesome will be the state of society

and the stronger the inner life of the individual.   The school must give to everybody that which binds us all in a common social intercourse, in an understanding of the public life and of nature.   The school would be hampered in this its highest mission if its program were encroached upon by the demands of personal calling.

But the dangers of a pseudo-professional work in the schools would result no less from the intrusion of an element of personal whim and fancy.   The child would follow his personal liking at a time when he needs most of all to learn to overcome his mere likes and dislikes. In the years that should be devoted to the learning of the highest task, the doing of one's duty, the boys and girls would be encouraged in the ruinous habit of following the path of least resistance.   The vocational aspect ought to be excluded absolutely from the public schools. Even subjects like manual training, which may become most useful for certain practical callings, in the schoolroom ought to be kept in the position of a formal discipline.   The boy should learn in his manual training lesson that power of accuracy and observation, of attention and energy, that will be helpful to him in every walk of life; he should not learn carpentry there in order to become a carpenter.   Truly, they are the youth's best friends who insist that this principle ought to hold even up to the higher stages of school life.   More elasticity may be allowed in the high school, and still more in the college work; but even these will ultimately be the more helpful the freer they are kept from professional aspects. Only when the schools have poured out their floods must the stream be guided into safe channels.

In the institution of vocational schools a most important step forward has been taken. Industrial education and trade schools have at last won the interest of progressive countries. By means of these perhaps more than by anything else, modern Germany has made its rapid strides forward. The boy of fourteen who cannot afford to prolong his general education can do no better than to get thorough instruction in a specialized line. The advantage of these vocational schools would have to be acknowledged without reservation if we did not face one serious danger. The school is excellent for the boy who would otherwise spend his time in a desultory bread-winning activity; but such a school is harmful if it draws the boy away from a further pursuit of liberal education. It would be most regrettable if the industrial schools should contribute still more to the growing depletion of the high schools. The vocational school is the desirable solution for those who cannot afford the higher school, but it is undesirable for those who, for practical reasons, prefer it to a further liberal training. Yet, if this danger is kept sufficiently in view, the blessing of the vocational school for the youth who is seeking a life work must be most heartily acknowledged.

Similar in importance is the establishment of vocation bureaus, a movement that was started in Boston by the late Professor Parsons, a true benefactor to the community, and

that has been taken up in various other places. It represents an innovation of unlimited possibilities. Parsons'
posthumous work on the choice of a vocation outlines his
plans and suggests vividly the manifold cases that have
been helped by the work of the vocation bureau. He recognized clearly that the need for guidance is at no time
in life more essential than in the transition from school to
work. He saw that inefficiency and change of vocation,
with all the waste and cost involved, " are largely due to
the haphazard way in which young men and women drift
into employments, with little or no regard to adaptability,
and without adequate preparation or any definite aim or
well-considered plan to insure success."

The effort of the vocation bureau is to remedy these conditions through expert counsel and guidance. The immediate means consist, first, in furnishing the young people
with a knowledge of the requirements and conditions of
success, the compensations, opportunities, and prospects in
different lines of work; second, in guiding the candidate to
a clear understanding of his own aptitudes, abilities, interests, resources, and limitations. Moreover, the officers of
the vocation bureau must act as true counselors, reasoning
patiently with the boy or girl on the practical relations between their personal qualities and those objective conditions
of the social fabric. Thus the goal of the bureau is to find
for every one the occupation that is in fullest harmony with
his nature and his ambitions and that will secure for him
the greatest possible permanent interest and economic
value. No doubt much depends upon the wisdom and

judgment, the sympathy and insight, of the counselor; and not every manager of such an institute will equal in that respect the founder of the first vocation bureau. Certainly, for such a task, thorough preparation is needed, and the equipment of a pioneer school for the training of vocational counselors was therefore necessarily the next step.

The gathering of objective data that are needed to furnish all possible information has been most successfully started, and the little guide-book already contains unusually rich material regarding the conditions of efficiency and success in different industries; a classification of industries; a most suggestive list of ways of earning money that are open to women at home and away from home, indoors and out of doors, skilled and unskilled. The bureau has also prepared schedules showing the earnings for each industry, the average wage, sex, and nativity of persons engaged in various occupations, the movement of demand in about two hundred vocations during the last decades, and many similar facts that would furnish the background for the discussion of any industrial case. All this becomes significant when applied to the personal qualifications of the candidate.

The methods employed to determine these individual facts are, so far, of a more tentative character. Here, decidedly, discussion is still open. And this is the point at which the interest of the experimental psychologist is attracted, and it appears his duty to take part in the discussion. The emphasis of the inquiry lies, as yet, on a self-analysis and on the impression of the counselor. In order to get the fullest possible self-analysis, the candidate is asked to answer, in writing, a large number of questions that refer to his habits and his emotions, his likings and his ambitions, his characteristics and his resources, his experiences and his capacities.   It seems in a high degree doubtful whether the results obtained by this method really throw a clear light on those mental factors that the counselor needs for his advice.   Such self-analysis is very difficult and, above all, very easily misleading.   The average man knows his mental functions as little as he knows the muscles that he uses in walking or speaking.   For instance, the boy is asked questions like the following:

Compare yourself as to courage with others of your age.
Is your attitude toward employers cordial and sympathetic or not?
If you could have your every wish fulfilled, what would be your first half dozen wishes?
What sort of people do you prefer to live with?
Mention the limitations and defects in yourself.
Do you cultivate smiles and laughter by right methods?
Do you take care to pronounce your words clearly?
Do you look people frankly in the eye?
Are you a good listener?
Are you thoughtful of the comfort of others?
Can you manage people well?
Are you planning to form further friendships?
Do you talk a good deal about yourself?
Are your inflections natural and cheery?

Such questions, representative of the most varied fields of inquiry, may yield bits of suggestion as to character in some cases, but they may, no less frequently, be answered misleadingly.   To estimate the value of his replies we should have to know the boy thoroughly; yet we seek those replies in order to get that thorough knowledge. Hence we move in a circle. If we desire a careful, exact analysis of mental functions, we must not forget that the last decades have brought the science of the mind to a point where such an analysis can be performed by means of an exact experimental science. The modern psychological laboratory disentangles the mental functions with a subtlety that surpasses the mere self-observation of practical life as much as the search with the microscope surpasses the viewing of objects with the naked eye.

It is true that the modern psychological laboratory has been interested primarily in the finding of general laws for the mental life. But in recent years the attention of experimental psychologists has turned more and more to the study of individual differences and to the development of methods designed to bring these differences to the clearest perception. We now realize that questions as to the mental capacities and functions and powers of an individual can no longer be trusted to impressionistic replies. If we are to have reliable answers, we must make use of the available resources of the psychological laboratory. These resources emancipate us from the illusions and emotions of the self-observer. The well-arranged experiment measures the mental states with the same exactness with which the chemical or physical examination of the physician studies the organism of the individual.

Of course, the psychological experiment does not enter into such complicated questions as those quoted. It turns to the elements of mental life.   And just here lies its strength.   As the organs of man are merely combinations of cells and tissues, so his mental personality is a complex combination of elementary states.   If we know the simple parts, we can calculate beforehand the fundamental direction of the development.   On the other hand, we can analyze every calling and vocation in order to find there, too, the essential elements and fundamental features.   We can determine which particular mental activities are needed for special lines of life work, and can then compare these demands with the table of results from an experimental analysis of the special mind.   Only the application of experimental tests can give to the advisory work that subtle adjustment by which discrimination between similar tasks becomes possible.

To give an illustration, there are mills in which everything depends on the ability of the workingman to watch, at the same time, a large number of moving shuttles, and to react quickly on a disturbance in any one.   The most industrious workman will be unsuccessful at such work if his attention is of the type that prevents him from such expansion of mental watchfulness.   The same man might be most excellent as a worker in the next mill, where the work demanded was dependent upon strong concentration of attention on one point.   There he would surpass his competitors just because he lacked expanded attention and had the focusing type.   The young man with an inclination to mill work does not know these differences, and his mere self-observation would never tell him whether his attention was of the expansive or of the concentrated type.

The psychological laboratory can test these individual differences of attention by a few careful experiments. The psychologist, therefore, is in a position to advise the youth at which type of factory to apply for work and which to avoid. Under present methods all would be largely a matter of chance. The man with the focusing attention might seek work in the mill where distributed attention is needed, and would feel sure that his industry and good will were sufficient to make him successful in his work. And yet the result would be disappointment and failure. Discouragement would ensue. He would soon lose his place, and drift on. The psychologist might have turned him in the right direction. The laboratory would have reproduced the essential characteristics of those various machines, and would have measured, perhaps in thousandth parts of a second, the rapidity, and in millimeters the accuracy, with which the reacting movements were performed at the various types of apparatus. These differences of attention are most important in various callings; and yet, the layman is inclined to discriminate only between good and bad attention. He is not aware that there exist a large variety of types of attention, each of which may be favorable for certain life works and very unfavorable for others.

To be sure, all such laboratory tests presuppose a real knowledge and careful analysis of the work to be performed.   Dilettantism here would easily lead into blind alleys.   I remember a case where the Boston Vocation Bureau asked me to examine the auditory reaction time of a young man who wanted to become a stenographer. The examination was to determine whether his response to sound was quicker or slower than the average.   If it were slower, he was to be warned against the career of a shorthand-writer.

I refused to undertake the test, because I considered that the conclusion would be misleading.   Even if the boy reacted slowly, so that the first word that he heard were written down by him possibly a fifth of a second later than his competitor wrote it, would that really show him to be less efficient?   If both were to write from dictation for a whole hour, the boy with the slower reaction time would still, at the end of the hour, be just a fifth of a second behind the other, which, of course, would be of no consequence.   The quickness of the other man's sound reaction would not make it at all certain that he would hold out with his shorthand-writing as long as the slower man.   In the imagination of the counselor, it appeared that the delay of a fifth of a second on the first word would bring an additional delay on the next word, and that the time lost would in this way accumulate.   What really needed to be examined was the rapidity of successive action and the retention in memory of the spoken words.

This problem of retention, too, demands very subtle inquiry.   The future stenographer knows that he needs a good memory, but to him the word " memory " covers mental functions that the psychologist must carefully separate. The young man confidently asserts that he has a good memory for words, because after a long interval he remembers what he has learned. Yet, that is an aspect of memory that is of no consequence for his shorthand work. The memory he needs is that of immediate retention. Experimental analyses demonstrate that this retention and the later remembering are two quite independent functions. For instance, the child has strong power of remembering, but small power of retention, while in the adult the power of retention surpasses that of remembering. The child must hear a number of words or figures more often than the adult before he can repeat them correctly. But, once the adult and the child have learned those figures, the chances are that the child will remember them after a longer time than the adult. The laboratory experimenter would always have to separate the test for such immediate reproduction from that for the later recall, and would have to consider carefully in which vocations the one or the other is an essential condition of success.

But if the psychological conditions of different vocations were scientifically disentangled and the mental analysis were carried through with all the discriminations that the progress of experimental psychology suggests, the vocation bureau would secure data that would be of the highest service. The association of ideas and the appreciation of the outer world, the imagination and the emotions, the feelings and the will, the attention and the discrimination, the accuracy and the effort, the suggestibility and the judgment, the persistence and the fatigue, the adaptability and the temperament, the skill, and even the character, with a hundred other functions and their interrelations, could be mapped out by decisive experiments. No boy ought to become a chauffeur, however his fancy is excited by motor-cars, if his reaction times in the laboratory indicate that he would not be quick enough to stop his automobile if a child ran in front of the wheels. No one ought to try for secretarial work who shows in the laboratory lack of inhibitory power and therefore a probable inability to be discreet. The boy who shows no sensitiveness for small differences ought not to work in a mill or factory in which his labor would be a constant repetition of the same activity. He would be oppressed by the uniformity of the work, it would soon be drudgery for him, and, with his interest, he would lose the good will. The next boy, who is sensitive to small differences, might find in the same work an inexhaustible pleasure and stimulus, as no two repetitions would be alike for him.

The other day I wired from Boston to a friend in another town that I should expect him the next day at the Hotel Somerset. The telegram arrived with the statement that I should be at the Hotel Touraine. The operator had substituted one leading hotel of Boston for another. No good will on his part can help that young man. He is not in the position of another Boston operator, whom I recently gave a cablegram to Berlin, and who, as he looked up the rate, asked: "Berlin is in France, isn't it?" The geography of the latter can be cured, but the mental mechanism of the former, who under pressure of rapid work substitutes an associated idea for the given one, is probably fundamental. The psychological laboratory would easily have found out such mental unreliability, and would have told the man beforehand that, however industrious he might be and however suited for a hundred other professions, that of the telegraph operator would not be one in which he could reach the fullest success.

The establishment of psychological laboratories as part of municipal vocation bureaus would by no means demand a very costly and elaborate outfit. An intelligent assistant with thorough psychological training could secure much of the material with a minimum of apparatus. There are hundreds of psychological experiments that can be carried out with some cardboard and sheets of paper, strings and pins and needles, little outline drawings and printed words, small colored tops and levers, hairpins and cardboard boxes, balls and boards, picture-books and smelling-bottles, a pack of cards and a set of weights and perhaps a cheap stop-watch. Where ampler funds are at the disposal of the bureau, an electrical chronoscope ought to be added, and, if possible, a kymograph. But in all cases the experiments themselves may be relatively simple, and even the most modest apparatus can furnish an abundance of insight into psychological differences of which the mere self-observation of the candidate does not take any account and for which any gaze of the outer observer would be insufficient.

The educational psychologists on the one side, the physicians, and especially the psychiatrists, on the other, have shown us the way in this field. The educator may ask a child to strike out the letter *e* wherever it occurs in a given page, and to do it as quickly as possible. He measures the time it requires and the accuracy with which it is done by seeing how often a wrong letter has been canceled and how often the right letter has been overlooked. He knows that even such a rapid test indicates more with regard to the attention and accuracy and swiftness of the child than he can find out by the regular school tests. He knows that only such elementary inquiries with exactly measureable results can discriminate between the various factors that are involved in any complex school work. Or the educator examines the power of the children to learn or to count at various hours of the day, and draws from it pedagogical conclusions as to the best arrangement of the school program. Of course, the school work must be adjusted to the average since all must have school work at the same time. Yet such experiments demonstrate the great individual differences. The curve of fatigue is different for almost every individual. Moreover, the psychological experiment can analyze the great varieties of fatigue, the fluctuations, the chances for a restitution of energy after fatigue; and it is evident that every result can be translated into advice or warning with regard to the vocational choice of the boy or girl. There are machines to which people with one type of fatigue could never be adapted, while those with another type might do excellent work.

Even the natural rhythm of motor functions is different for every individual. The pace at which we walk or speak or write is controlled by organic conditions of our will, and is hardly open to any complete change. Again, it is clear that the thousands of technical occupations demand very different rhythms of muscle contraction. If a man of one natural rhythmical type has to work at a machine that demands a very different rhythmical pace, life will be a perpetual conflict in which irritation and dissatisfaction with his own work will spoil his career and will ruin his chances for promotion. In a similar way, simple experiments might determine the natural lines of interest in a boy or girl. We might show pictures of farms or factories, of ships or railroads, of mines or banks, of natural scenery or street scenes, of buildings or theater stages, and so on. How much is kept in memory and how much is correctly apperceived after an exposure of a few seconds, how they affect the emotional expressions, and similar observations of objective character, may quickly point to mental traits that must be considered if a harmonious life work is to be hoped for.

There is no fear that such institutes, with their psychological laboratories, would play the guardian in too rigid and mechanical a way, restricting too much the natural freedom of the youth. On the contrary, nothing but the counselor's advice would be intended, and no one who was unwilling to listen to a warning would be restrained from following his own inclination.

The young genius will always find his way alone, and even his severe disappointments are a beneficial part of his schooling for higher service; but the great average masses do not know this powerful inner energy that magnetically draws the mind toward the ideal goal. They do not know the world and its demands; they do not know the opportunities and the rewards, the dangers and the difficulties; and they do not know themselves, their powers and their limitations. The old Greek legend tells us that when a man and woman find each other for life, it is a reuniting of two separate halves that have been one whole in a previous existence. This ought to be the way in which a man and his profession might find each other. But not every marriage nowadays suggests the Greek legend, and the unity of vocation and individual seems still less often predestined. And if fate has not decided the union in such a previous life, society ought at least to take care that in this life the choice be made with open eyes and with the advice of a counselor who knows how to fructify the psychological knowledge of our age.

III

THE STANDING OF SCHOLARSHIP

III

THE STANDING OF SCHOLARSHIP

A LL signs seem to point in the same direction. From the primary school to the university, from the kindergarten to the vocational life, there seems to arise in our day a demand for greater thoroughness and effort and serious concentration. A hundred symptoms indicate, and serious educators proclaim, that a turn of the road is near. There may have been a time — perhaps it is only a legend — when education had become ineffective through its formalism and rigidity. The children were forced by severe methods to do work repugnant to them. The prescribed studies of the college boys were dry and tiresome. It must have been a depressing kind of instruction in which the best energies of the youth were insistently subdued. A great reaction had to come. School-time was to be made a period of happiness, the child was to learn only what he liked, the college boy was to study only that which seemed interesting. Only that which appealed to the taste and to the attention was deemed worthy of the classroom. Instead of formal training, at last we had instruction which really opened to the boys and girls a gay-colored world where they might enjoy themselves to their heart's content. It was

47

a period in which the children were no longer ordered, but begged and persuaded; in which the abundance of elective courses made a handsome volume out of the announcements of the smallest college; athletics flourished, and in the school all, with the exception of the teachers, had a good time.

But now in the zigzag movement of educational progress, a new counter-movement seems imminent. We have been trying the national experiment long enough to test its results. We have seen the girls who have been educated in the high schools with " current events," and the boys who were no longer molested by the demand for Greek. But the outcome seemed more disappointing than ever. Every one who was not deceived by a showy exterior soon discovered the mental flabbiness and superficiality which resulted from the go-as-you-please methods. We began to feel that those who had never learned to obey never really became their own masters; those who had never trained their attention by forcing their will toward that which is unattractive had to learn by severe disappointments later that a large part of every life's work must be drudgery. The youth left the school with a hundred things in their minds, but without any power of intellectual self-discipline.

Our public life reflects this lack everywhere. The newspapers and magazines, the theaters and the social-reform movements, are more and more made for a public which looks only to be entertained, and which has lost the power of sustained attention to that which is not attractive in itself; and the nation slowly begins to realize that such a mental state of the community is the natural soil of every kind of moral weed.   Thoroughness is only another form of conscientiousness. He who early acquires the habit of inaccuracy and carelessness will never have the energy to work against evil where it is easier and more convenient to let things go as they will.

We stand only at the beginning of this new reaction, but we already hear from many sides that more serious discipline and training and effort must be secured.   This coincides with the fact that educational psychology, since it has entered into the stage of careful experimental work, has brushed away the widespread prejudices regarding the training of mental powers.   The theorists who advocated the coddling education had made much of the fact that no training can really change the mental powers of the individual.   A bad memory never becomes a good one. Experimental psychology has demonstrated the fallacy of such pet ideas.   Memory and attention, apperception and reasoning, feeling and emotion, effort and will, can be remoulded by a well-directed education; and this development of the mental powers may easily appear to many as a more important gain than any addition to the stored-up knowledge of facts.   But the community on the whole is not eager to consult the experimental psychologist: from the deepest needs of social life the new longing has arisen.

If the nation is not to suffer by a cheap complacency and the triumph of ostentatious mediocrity, the whole educational life must be filled with a new spirit of devotion to serious tasks. The commencement addresses of the leading men of the country this year have given fervent expression to this instinctive demand of the nation. So far as the colleges are concerned, one imperative change stands in the center of every platform: scholarship must receive a more dignified standing in the eyes of the undergraduates. The constant appeal to the mere liking of child and boy and adolescent has finally made the sideshows more important than the real arena. The university administrations practically everywhere recognize such a reform as a most urgent need. Means must be found to effect a complete revision in the views of the average students. So long as the best human material in our colleges considers it as more or less below its level to exert effort on its studies; so long as it gladly leaves the high marks to the second-rate grinds, and considers it the part of a real gentleman to spend four college years with work done well enough not to be dismissed, and poorly enough never to excel, there is something vitally wrong in the academic atmosphere.

Some seem inclined to think that the whole blame belongs to athletics. If the interest in intercollegiate sport is allowed to take hysteric character, and if the successful college athlete stands in the limelight of publicity, it appears necessary that the devotee of quiet scholarship should remain unnoticed in the dark, and that his modest career should not attract the energetic fellow. Whatever the reasons may be, many suggestions for reform have been made. Perhaps none may more quickly lead to an improvement than the much-discussed plan of introducing a stronger element of competition into the scholarly sphere, and thus using for intellectual purposes those levers which have been so effective in the field of sport. The effort to put the highest energy into scholarship has not reached its ideal form so long as it is controlled by the hope of surpassing a rival. That for which we must aim is certainly a more genuine enthusiasm for intellectual efficiency. And yet the present situation would not only excuse, but really demand, the fullest possible play of these secondary motives. If we can foster scholarship by an appeal to the spirit of rivalry, by all means let us use it. We may hope that as soon as better traditions have been formed, and higher opinions have been spread, the interest in the serious work will replace the motives of vanity. As soon as the finest men of the college turn, from whatever motives, with their full strength toward their class-work, the masses may follow, and higher and higher ambitions will be developed.

Of course, no one can overlook some intrinsic difficulties in the way of such plans. No artificial premium can focus on the successful scholar that same amount of flattering interest and notoriety which the athletic victory easily yields. The difference lies simply in the fact that the student's athletic achievement represents, in that little field, a performance which may be compared with the very best. The scholarly work of the undergraduate, on the other hand, at its highest point necessarily remains

nothing but a praiseworthy exercise, incomparable with
the achievement of great scholars.   The student football-
player may win a world's record; the student scholar in
the best case may justify noble hopes, but his achievement will be surpassed by professional scholars every
day.

But the real difficulties in the transformation of the
present state, after all, lie much deeper.   Certainly, the
faculties of the universities ought not to leave anything
undone which may shift the center of gravity in the little
encircled academic world.   But however high the hopes
may be, we ought not to underestimate the much greater
difficulties which have their origin outside of this college
world.   May it not be an illusion to believe that the de-
plorable lack of appreciation for scholarship of students
can ever be fundamentally changed so long as the corresponding ideas in the great world outside of the college
campus are not thoroughly revised?   No college faculty
can change situations on the campus, if they are simply
symptoms and results of the conditions in our whole social
organization.   The scholarship of the students will never
be fully appreciated by the most vital men in college so
long as public opinion does not back them; that is, so
long as scholarship has no real standing in the American
community.

If we are sincere, we ought not to overlook the fact
that the scholar, as such, has no position in public opinion
which corresponds to the true value of his achievement.
The foreigner feels at once this difference between the

Americans and the Europeans. The other day we mourned the death of Simon Newcomb. There seems to be a general agreement that astronomy is the one science in which America has been in the first rank of the world, and that Newcomb was the greatest American astronomer. Yet his death did not bring the slightest ripple of excitement. The death of the manager of the professional baseball games interested the country rather more. Public opinion did not show the slightest consciousness of an incomparable loss at the hour when the nation's greatest scholar closed his eyes. And if I compare it with that deep national mourning with which the whole German nation grieved at the loss of men like Helmholtz and Mommsen and Virchow, and many another, the contrast becomes most significant.

When the president of Harvard University gave up his administrative work, the old Harvard students and the whole country enthuisastically brought to him the highest thanks which he so fully deserved. But when, the year before, William James left Harvard, the most famous scholar who has worked in this Harvard generation, the event passed by like a routine matter. At the commencement festivities every speaker spoke of the departing administrative officer, but no one thought of the departing scholar. And that exactly expresses the general feeling.

It was said with emphasis the other day that the strength of the American university lies in its graduates. In Germany, for instance, inside and outside of the academic circles, every one would take it as a matter of course that the strength of a university lies exclusively in the professors; and moreover in the professors as scholars. If I think back to my student days in my fatherland, the greatest events of those happy years were the festivities and torchlight processions which we boys organized for our great professors when they declined a call to another university. Their work and their fame in the world of scholarship was our greatest pride. For their sake we had selected one or another alma mater. The American students feel this pride and attachment only for the institution as such; the individual scholars there are to them merely the appointed teachers; they may like them as teachers, but consider their scholarly achievment a private affair.

A very characteristic symptom of the situation is the prevalent opinion that as a matter of course every professor is ready to become a college president. Again and again scholars from most widely different fields are discussed for presidencies, even in places where they would have to give up their scholarly work and be obliged to go over entirely into administrative work. It is evident that such a change lies well in the line of men whose scholarship refers to government or economics or similar subjects. But if a scholar of Greek or mathematics is treated as an equally natural candidate, it clearly indicates that the public does not consider the university professor primarily as a productive scholar, but essentially as an officer of the institution. To change from a professorship to a presidency then appears as a kind of promotion, while in reality it means a change of profession.

In both the United States and Germany the scholars are almost exclusively university professors, in striking contrast to France and England, where many of the greatest scholars have always been outside of the universities. But this personal union has had different effects in the two countries. In Germany, the exultant respect for scholarship raised the career of the mere university professor; in America, by the lack of respect for scholarship, the standing of the individual scholar has on the whole come to be determined by his administrative position in the universities. Those who have a kind of personal reputation, independent of their services to the institutions, owe it as a rule to extraneous features. Perhaps they make a practical discovery, or give eloquent popular lectures, master a picturesque epigrammatic style or like to write magazine articles in their leisure hours; in a word, they earn a reputation by their by-products, in spite of their scholarship.

Again, it would be shortsighted to isolate this feature of public opinion from the whole social physiognomy. This relatively low standing of the scholar's work very naturally resulted from the whole make-up of public opinion. It is certainly not a necessary part of democracy, but it has been a characteristic element in the development of American public life, that every one feels himself a judge of everything, every one is fit for every place, and every one knows what is worth while in life. There is no one who can appeal so little to such a court of judges as the scholar. He has nothing to show. Even the greatest scholar could not point to a fair success, when the success is to be measured in commercial terms. Any clever lawyer or skillful physician would greatly outshine him — not to speak of the banker and the broker. He cannot show his success in that popularity of notoriety which comes to the politician or the literary man or the administrator or the athlete. His work interests a few score of colleagues. Even the external conditions do not furnish those official labels by which the high opinion of the few who know is made widely visible to the crowd — the English knighthood for the leading scholars, the governmental decorations and titles. Men whose names may be among the noblest assets of the United States in future centuries, at a time when the names of the wheat kings and railroad kings will be forgotten, thus remain negligible quantities in the public opinion of to-day.

Hence the most direct reflection of this public situation in the college life is not the disrespect for high-grade class-work, but, still more, the unwillingness of the best men to turn toward a scholarly career. It seems to be the unanimous experience of the faculties in all the leading universities that the men who turn to the graduate school represent a less energetic material than the average of the senior class or of the law school. The finest men go into business and industry, law and medicine; and those who turn to the graduate schools of the country to pursue the life of a scholar are, in the majority, men without initiative and ambition, and without promise for the highest kind of work. Of course, there is no lack of exceptions. There will always be a few men whose genius calls them, who feel the need of solving the problems which are before their souls, and whose vision sees clearly the noble scholarly achievement. But these exceptions are too few. The man with power and ambition usually seeks another path, he cannot feel attracted to a calling which finds so little appreciation in the community, he must instinctively feel as if he were going into a second-rate profession in which no high rewards are awaiting him. And all this constitutes a vicious circle, with the common result that in all layers of society, with young and old alike, scholarship is not acknowledged as a vital force. It has no access to the inner life of men.

The world laughed when Heinrich Heine's disrespectful humor in the *Harzreise* ridiculed the scholarly pedantry of old Göttingen. He says, " Before the gate of the town I heard two little schoolboys, and the one said to the other, ' I no longer want to have any social intercourse with Theodore. He is a disgusting cheap fellow. Yesterday he did not even know the genitive of *mensa.*' " Yes: that sounds absurd; and yet there will never be really great scholarship in a country where there is not sufficient honor for scholarship to attract the very best men to such a career; and the adult men will never possess this high belief, unless the whole atmosphere is so filled with it that even the children instinctively feel it.

Yet the fact that scholarship has no worthy standing in the community at large is again not the ultimate source of the distortion of values. We must go still further to find what is really the last sociological cause. Behind all of it stands a characteristic view of life, a kind of philosophy which is on the whole vaguely felt, but which not seldom even comes to definite expression. Whenever it becomes shaped in such definite form, it is proclaimed, not as a debatable proposition, and not as an argument which is upheld against any possible opposition, but it is always naïvely presented as a matter-of-course principle. This naïve philosophizing crystallizes about the one idea that the end of all social striving is to be the happiness of individuals. Now, this is exactly the well-meaning philosophy of the eighteenth century, the philosophy of the rationalists in the period of enlightenment. It is a philosophy which formed the background of all the social movements of that important period, and was therefore the philosophy out of which the Constitution of the United States naturally arose.

The greatest happiness of the greatest number of individuals is indeed the social ideal which, outspoken or not, controls the best forward movements of the country. It seems to stand above the need of any defense, as it evidently raises itself high above the low selfishness of the masses. He who works for the pleasures of millions must be in the right, because those who think only of their own pleasure are certainly in the wrong. Now, to be sure, a social body organized in order to secure the maximum of happiness for its members will have a high appreciation of knowledge. The period of enlightenment very naturally even overestimated the value of knowledge as an equipment of man. But knowledge then and now was in question only as a tool for practical achievement. Such a society will therefore work with the greatest enthusiasm for good schools and widespread education, and will take care that everybody may have the opportunity to learn as much as possible, because wide information and acquaintance with the world must help the individual in his striving for individual success and satisfaction. The splendid efforts of the American people for the raising and expanding of the school system are thus completely in line with this latent philosophy of enlightenment.

But the history of civilization shows that such philosophy is by no means a matter of course; it is a particular aspect seen from a particular standpoint. Other periods, other nations, have seen the world from other standpoints, and have emphasized other aspects of reality. In a bird's-eye view we see throughout the history of mankind the fluctuations and alternations between positivism and idealism. The philosophy of enlightenment is positivism. It is true, in the trivial talk of the street, we call a man an idealist if he does not think of his personal profit, but of the pleasure of his neighbors. But, in a higher sense of the word, such unselfish altruism does not constitute an idealistic view of the world. On the contrary, it may have all the earmarks of positivism.

We have positivism wherever the concrete experiences — and that means that which " is "— make up the whole of reality. We have idealism where the view of the world is controlled by a belief in absolute values for which there is no " is," but only an " ought; " which have not the character of concrete experiences, but the meaning of obligations which are to be fulfilled, not in the interest of individuals, but on account of their absolute value. For the positivist, knowledge and truth and beauty and progress and morality have meaning merely in so far as they contribute to the concrete experiences of satisfaction in existing individuals: for the idealist, they represent ideals the realization of which gives meaning to individual life, but is eternally valuable independent of the question whether their fulfillment contributes to the pleasure of individuals. From such an idealistic point of view it seems shallow and meaningless to see the end of striving in a larger amount of individual happiness. The purpose of man is to do his duty,— not to be pleased.

This is not the place to enter into a real discussion of these two types of philosophy, and to develop the system of eternal values as against the relativism and pragmatism and utilitarianism of the positivists. This is not even the place to ask which of the two views of the world, and of human life, is the deeper one and the more fit to give account of the reality in which we live. Here we have to emphasize only the fact that this great antagonism of world-views is going on, in order to insist that scholarship, that is, the devotion to the advancement of knowledge, can find its true appreciation only in a society which instinctively believes in idealism.

To give at once a historical background to this contrast, we have only to look from the philosophy of the United States to the underlying world-view of the German nation. Germany went through the same ideas of enlightenment in the eighteenth century; then came the great philosophical-literary uplifting of the national spirit, the period of Schiller and Goethe, of Kant and Fichte and Hegel. It was a national reorganization, in which the idea of the purpose of man became thoroughly revised. Not experience, but conviction; not the " is," but the " ought," became the pivot. This does not mean that the average man read, or would have understood, Kant and Fichte; but the ideas of the great thinkers reached the entire national life through a thousand channels, and the whole new German education and organization of society was controlled by this idealistic turn. Duty and discipline and submission to an ideal of absolute value became the underlying forces; and, however much millions of selfish individuals may have wandered away from the ideal, the fundamental direction of the national energies had been given.

The aim of life then became the realization of absolute values. The individual and the state alike received through this conviction their aim and their meaning; and nothing else can claim real dignity but that which ultimately serves this ideal fulfillment. In such a philosophy the moral deed is not valuable because it adds to the pleasure of the neighbor, but because it is eternally good; the work of art is valuable, not because it pleases the senses, but because it realizes the ideal of beauty; the world of the market is valuable, not because it satisfies individual needs, but because it means a realization of the ideal of progress; the life of the state is valuable, not because it secures the greatest happiness of its members, but because it is a realization of the ideals of right, and as such of eternal value: and knowledge, too, is valuable, not because it is a serviceable tool for the pleasure of individuals, but because it is a fulfillment of the ideal of truth.

In a society in which this is the instinctive background of public feeling, the incomparable position of scholarship must be secure from the start. The scholar, like the artist or the minister or the statesman, serves his ideal with every fibre of his life. Whether his knowledge will ever be transformed into practical use for anything is not the question. That could not add to the worth and dignity of his achievement. All which gives meaning and absolute value to his creation is that it serves the advancement of truth, that it adds to the world's forward movement toward the ideal. The scholar, as productive scholar, therefore stands on a higher level than he who serves only the happiness of individuals. Where such a thought, clearly expressed or vaguely implied, stands in the center of national ideas, it must be reflected everywhere; it must give to every effort toward knowledge a new meaning and a new aspiration. To learn for truth's sake then becomes a kind of ideal service; and even if it is indeed only the genitive of *mensa*, it means duty.

Such an idealistic view of the world may seem and must seem to many a logical monstrosity. They have their skeptical and positivistic and pragmatic arguments on the tip of their tongues. And this antagonism has existed at all times. There would have been no need for a Socrates and a Plato and their idealism, if the country had not resounded with the positivism of the old Sophists. The point is only that we must not believe that, in a positivistic, utilitarian society, we can ever give that standing to scholarship which it naturally has in a society controlled by philosophical idealism. Of course, many would say that a change would not be worth while anyhow, or that it would be too dearly bought, if we were to get higher standing for scholarship and government and art by giving up our philosophy of enlightenment. But it must be clear that we cannot have one without the other. And at least we ought to give up the superficial illusion that just such a type of positivistic philosophy is the regulation equipment for a true democracy.

Indeed, there is no lack of indications that American life, too, is trying to overcome the narrowness of utilitarian philosophy, and is moving toward idealistic ground; nothing seems to hold back this progress so much as the illusion that the greatest happiness of the individual is the only possible goal for a democracy. On the surface it may appear as if positivism has more consideration for every concrete individual, and is thus more inclined to

award an equal share of the world's pleasures to every
one. On the other hand, idealism, which believes in the
value of the whole as a whole, may appear more inclined
to appreciate the symbols which represent the whole, and
therefore to endorse the symbolic forms of the monarchy.
In this sense it was not by chance that the Americans,
under the influence of a positivistic philosophy of the
eighteenth century, founded a republic.

Yet history shows that utilitarian motives have erected
monarchies too, and that true democracies have been
filled with the spirit of idealism. The American attitude
there is controlled by nothing but tradition. Their
democracy originated historically from a positivistic philosophy which was most suitable for a century of pioneer-
ing and developing the resources of the new world. But
now, as times have changed, as new aims and historic
purposes come into the foreground, the national philosophy too must adjust itself to the new age; and progress
ought not to be hampered by an illusory belief in the
democratic character of utilitarianism. On the contrary,
if the purpose of life is understood as the realization of
ideals, the democracy comes to its highest meaning.
Each man has an ideal share in the national duty, each
man equally should contribute his part toward the realization of absolute values, and equally should submit his
individual desire for his pleasure and happiness, for his
individual fancy and opinion, to the service of the ideal
good.

There is an abundance of factors which, even in the

midst of our utilitarian life, point to the necessity of this inner change. For instance, it is very curious to see how the technical complexity of our life forces on individuals an increasing submission to the judgment of the expert. At first it was only the expert in engineering and sanitation, slowly it has become the expert in education, finally it will become the expert in government. But whether the positivism of the time will be undermined by such new practical demands, or by new philosophical thoughts, or by a new emotional revival, in any case indications are abundantly visible that a change is to come. This great new educational uprising against the go-as-you-please scheme, and this new cry for more thoroughness and discipline, for more serious respect for scholarship, are after all only symptoms of this great national movement. It is essential to recognize these connections. So long as the reforms are confined to our school and our colleges, they may improve the situation but can never be fundamentally effective. The real reform can come only if it is supported by a corresponding movement throughout the national life.

As soon as the nation feels that the meaning of life lies, not in the greatest pleasure for the greatest number of individuals, but in the realization of eternal ideals, then, as a matter of course, school and college and vocational life will be reshaped and reorganized. Then, on the university campus, scholarship and athletics will no longer be rivals which stand on the same level: athletics will be the joyful play which gives pleasure and recreation to individuals, and serves its purpose well if it makes happy boys more able to live for their real life-tasks; but scholarship will be a service which does not ask but which finds respect everywhere, as it is sacred through its own dignity. Service to scholarship will then appear to every one just as valuable as honesty and morality; it is an eternal reward in itself.

IV

PROHIBITION AND TEMPERANCE

IV

PROHIBITION AND TEMPERANCE

IF a German stands up to talk about prohibition, he
might just as well sit down at once, for every one in
America, of course, knows beforehand what he is going
to say. Worse, every one knows also exactly why he is
so anxious to say it: how can he help being on the wrong
side of this question? And especially if he has been a
student in Germany, he will have brought the drinking
habit along with him from the Fatherland, together with
his cigar smoking and card playing and duelling. If a
man relies on his five quarts of heavy Munich beer a day,
how can he ever feel happy if he is threatened with no
license in his town and with no beer in his stein? Yet
my case seems slightly different. I never in my life
played cards, I never fought a duel, and when the other
day in a large women's college, after an address and a
reception, the lady president wanted to comfort me and
suggested that I go into the next room and smoke a cigar,
I told her frankly that I could do it if it were the rule in
her college, but that it would be my first cigar. With
beer it is different. Last winter in traveling I was for
some days the guest of an Episcopal clergyman, who, an-
ticipating the visit of a German, had set up a bottle of

beer as a welcome, and we drank together the larger part
of the bottle — but I think that is my only case in late
years.   When I had to attend a Students' "Commers,"
I was always protected by the thick mug through which
no one could discover that the contents never became less
during the evening.   I live most comfortably in a pleasant temperance town which will, I hope, vote no-license
year by year as long as freshmen stroll over the old Harvard Yard.   And although I have become pretty much
Americanized, I have never drunk a cocktail.

Hence the problem of prohibition does not affect my
thirst, but it greatly interests my scientific conscience; not
as a German, but as a psychologist I feel impelled to add
a word to the discussion which is suddenly reverberating
over the whole country.   But is it really a discussion
which we hear?   Is it not rather a one-sided denunciation
of alcohol, repeated a million times with louder and
louder voice, an outcry ever swelling in its vehemence?
On the other side there may be the protests of the distillers and brewers and wine-growers and bottle-makers
and saloon-keepers, and perhaps some timid declarations
of thirsty societies — but such protests do not count, since
they have all the earmarks of selfishness; they are ruled
out, and no one listens, just as no one would consult the
thieves if a new statute against pickpockets were planned.
So far as the really disinterested public is concerned, the
discussion is essentially one-sided.   If serious men like
Cardinal Gibbons raise their voices in a warning against

prohibition, they are denounced and overborne, and no one cares to imitate them.

It has been seldom indeed that the fundamental evil of American public opinion has come out so clearly; namely, that no one dares to be on the unpopular side; just as in fashion and social life, every one wants to be "in it." No problem in America has a fair hearing as soon as one side has become the fashion of mind. Only the cranks come out with an unbalanced, exaggerated opposition and thus really help the cause they want to fight against. The well-balanced thinkers keep quiet and simply look on while the movement rushes forward, waiting quietly for the reaction which sets in from the inner absurdity of every social extreme. The result is too often a zigzag movement, where fearlessness might have found a middle way of steady progress. There must be indeed a possible middle way between the evil of the present saloon and the no less evil of a future national prohibition; yet if this one-sidedness of discussion goes on, it is not difficult to foresee, after the legislative experiences of the last years, that the hysterical movement will not stop until prohibition is proclaimed from every state-house between the Atlantic and the Pacific.

Exaggerated denunciation of the prohibition movement is, of course, ineffective. Whoever simply takes sides with the saloon-keeper and his clientèle — yes, whoever is blind to the colossal harm which alcohol has brought and is now bringing to the whole country — is unfit to be heard by those who have the healthy and sound development of the nation at heart. The evils which are connected with the drinking habit are gigantic; thousands of lives and many more thousands of households are the victims every year; disease and poverty and crime grow up where alcohol drenches the soil. To deny it means to ignore the teachings of medicine and economics and criminology.

But is this undeniable fact really a proof of the wisdom of prohibition? The railroads of the United States injured last year more than one hundred thousand persons and put out seven thousand hopeful lives; does any sane man argue that we ought to abolish railroads? The stock exchange has brought recently, economic misery to uncounted homes, but even at the height of the panic no one wanted to destroy the market for industrial stocks. To say that certain evils come from a certain source suggests only to fools the hasty annihilation of the source before studying whether greater evils might not result from its destruction, and without asking whether the evils might not be reduced, and the good from the same source remain untouched and untampered with. Even if a hollow tooth aches, the modern dentist does not think of pulling it; that would be the remedy of the clumsy village barber. The evils of drink exist, and to neglect their cure would be criminal, but to rush on to the conclusion that every vineyard ought therefore to be devastated is unworthy of the logic of a self-governing nation. The other side has first to show its case.

This does not mean that every argument of the other

side is valid. In most of the public protestations, especially from the Middle West, far too much is made of the claim that all the Puritanic laws and the whole prohibitionist movement are an interference with personal liberty. It is an old argument, indeed, " Better England free than England sober." For public meetings it is just the kind of protest which resounds well and rolls on nobly. We are at once in the midst of the " most sacred " rights. Who desires that America, the idol of those who seek freedom from the tyranny of the Old World, shall trample on the right of personal liberty? And yet those hundreds of singing-societies which have joined in this outburst of moral indignation have forgotten that every law is a limitation of personal liberty. The demand of the nation must limit the demands of the individual, even if it is not the neighbor, but the actor himself who is directly hurt. No one wants to see the lottery or gambling-houses or the free sale of morphine and cocaine permitted, or slavery, even though a man were to offer himself for sale, or polygamy, even though all wives should consent. To prevent temptation toward ruinous activities is truly the State's best right, and no injury to personal liberty. The German reflects gladly how much more the German State apparently intrudes upon personal freedom: for instance, in its splendid State insurance for old age and accidents.

To be sure, from this German viewpoint it is hard to understand why the right of the State to subordinate personal wishes to national ones should not carry with it a duty to make compensation.   To him the actions of some Southern States appear simply as the confiscation of property.   When, as has happened, a captain of industry erects a most costly brewery, and the State in the following year prohibits the sale of beer, turning the large, new establishment into a huge, useless ruin, without giving the slightest compensation, the foreigner stands aghast, wondering if to-morrow a party which believes in the State ownership of railroads may not prohibit railroading by private companies without any payment to the present owners.

Yet the political aspect does not concern the social psychologist.   I abstract from it as from many others. There is, indeed, no limit to the problems which ought to be studied most seriously before such a gigantic revolution is organized.   The physician may ask whether and when alcohol is real medicine, and the physiologist may study whether it is a food and whether it is rightly taken as helpful to nutrition; but this is not our problem.   The theologians may quarrel as to whether the Bible praises the wine or condemns the drinker, whether Christ really turned water into that which we call wine, and whether Christianity as such stands for abstinence.   It is matter for the economist to ask what will become of the hundreds of thousands of men who are working to-day in the breweries and related industries.   A labor union claims that " over half a million men would be thrown out of employment by general prohibition, who, with their families, would make an army of a million human beings robbed of

their means of existence." And the economist, again,
may consider what it might mean to take out the license
taxes from the city budgets and the hundreds of millions
of internal revenue from the budget of the whole country.
It is claimed that the breweries, maltsters, and distillers
pay out for natural and manufactured products, for labor,
transportation, etc., seven hundred million dollars an-
nually; that their aggregate investments foot up to more
than three thousand millions; and that their taxes contribute three hundred and fifty millions every year to the
public treasuries.   Can the country afford to ruin an industry of such magnitude?   Such weighty problems cannot be solved in the Carrie Nation style: yet they are
not ours here.

Nearer to our psychological interest comes the well-
known war-cry, " Prohibition does not prohibit." It is
too late in the day to need to prove it by statistics: every
one knows it.   No one has traveled in prohibition States
without seeing the sickening sight of drunkards of the
worst order.   The drug-stores are turned into very re-
munerative bars, and through hidden channels whiskey and
gin flood the community.   The figures of the United States
Commissioner of Internal Revenue tell the story publicly.   In a license State like Massachusetts, there exists
one retail liquor dealer for every 525 of population; in a
prohibition State like Kansas, one for every 366.   But
the secret story is much more alarming.   What is the
effect?   As far as the health of the nation and its mental
training in self-control and in regulation of desires are

concerned, the result must be dangerous, because, on the whole, it eliminates the mild beverages in favor of the strong drinks and substitutes lonely drinking for drinking in social company. Both are psychologically and physiologically a turn to the worse. It is not the mild beer and light wine which are secretly imported; it is much easier to transport and hide whiskey and rum, with their strong alcoholic power and stronger effect on the nerve-cells of the brain. And of all forms of drinking none is more ruinous than the solitary drink, as soon as the feeling of repugnance has been overcome; there is no limit and no inhibition. If I look back over the last years, in which I often studied the effects of suggestion and hypnotism on habitual drinkers, I do not hesitate to say that it was in most cases easier to cure the social drinker of the large cities, than to break the lonely drinker of the temperance town. Of course, prohibition reduces somewhat the whole quantity of consumption, but it withdraws the stimulant, in most cases, where it would do the least harm and intensifies the harm to the organism where it is most dangerous.

But man is not only a nervous system. Prohibition forced by a majority on an unwilling minority will always remain a living source of the spirit of disregard for law. Yet, " unwilling " minority is too weak an epithet; the question is of a minority which considers the arbitrary rule undemocratic, absurd, immoral, and which really believes that it is justified in finding a secret way around a contemptible law.

Judges know how rapidly the value of the oath sinks in courts where violation of the prohibition laws is a frequent charge, and how habitual perjury becomes tolerated by respected people. The city politicians know still better how closely blackmail and corruption hang together, in the social psychology, with the enforcement of laws that strike against the beliefs and traditions of wider circles. The public service becomes degraded, the public conscience becomes dulled. And can there be any doubt that disregard of law is the most dangerous psychological factor in our present-day American civilization? It is not lynch law which is the worst; the crimes against life are twenty times more frequent than in Europe, and as for the evils of commercial life which have raised the wrath of the whole well-meaning nation in late years, has not disregard of law been their real source? In a popular melodrama the sheriff says solemnly: " I stand here for the law "; and when the other shouts in reply, " I stand for common sense! " night after night the public breaks out into jubilant applause. To foster this immoral negligence of law by fabricating hasty, ill-considered laws in a hysterical mood, laws which almost tempt toward a training in violation of them, is surely a dangerous experiment in social psychology.

Hasty indeed is that kind of law-making. Within a few years, during which the situation itself has not been changed, during which no new discoveries have proved the right or necessity, during which no experts have reached common results, the wave has swollen to a devastating flood. Who let it loose? Were the psychologists asked to decide, or the physicians, or the physiologists, or the sociologists, or any one who has studied the problem as a whole with professional knowledge? Certainly not: their commissions have hardly ever proposed total abstinence. Of course, those who rush on mean the best as they see it; they want to make better men; but can a nation ever hope to reach private morality by law and thus to exclude all private lying and greediness and envy and ingratitude and temper and unfairness just as well as intemperance? Such vague mixing of purposes always characterizes superficial legislation. A sober contemplator must ask himself: What is it to lead to if well-meaning, short-sighted dilettantes can force legislation on questions which demand the most serious expert study?

There is growing throughout the land to-day a conviction — which has its core of truth — that many people eat too much meat; and not a few see a remedy in vegetarianism and Fletcherism. If this prejudice swells in a similar way, the time may come when one State after the other will declare slaughtering illegal, confiscate the meat-packing houses, and prohibit the poisonous consumption of beef and the killing of any creature that can look on us with eyes. Other groups are fighting coffee and tea, and we may finally land in nuts and salads. Yes, according to this line of legislative wisdom, there is no reason for prohibiting only alcohol. Do I go far beyond the facts in asserting that in certain States the same women and men who are publicly against every use of

alcohol are also opposed to the " drugs " of the physicians and speak of them privately as poisons? Not the
Christian Scientists only — in intellectual Boston thousands of educated women speak of drugs and nervine as
belonging to a medieval civilization which they have outgrown.   The same national logic may thus lead us to laws
which will prohibit every physician from using the resources of the drug-store — unless they are all compelled
to go over to osteopathy.

The question of the liquor trade and temperance —
which is so widely different from a hasty prohibition —
has engaged the minds of all times and of all nations, and
is studied everywhere to-day with the means of modern
science. But this spring flood of prohibition legislation
which has overrun the States shows few signs of deeper
connection with serious study and fewer signs of profit
from the experiments of the past.   When the Chinese
government made laws against intemperance about eleven
hundred years before Christ, it can hardly have gone more
hastily to work than the members of this movement of the
twentieth century after Christ.   It is unworthy of women
and men who want to stand for sobriety to allow themselves to become intoxicated with hysterical outcries, when
a gigantic national question is to be solved, a question
which can never be solved until it is solved rightly.   A
wrong decision must necessarily lead to a social reaction
which can easily wipe out every previous gain.

Progress is to be hoped for only from the most careful analysis of all the factors of this problem; yet, instead,

the nation leaves it to the unthinking, emotional part of the population. In the years of the silver agitation the wonderful seriousness with which large crowds listened in a hundred towns, evening after evening, to long hours of difficult technical discussion on currency was a matter of admiration to any foreigner. Sixteen to one was really discussed by the whole nation, and arguments were arrayed against arguments before a decision was reached. Is it necessary that the opposite method be taken as soon as this problem is touched — a question far more complex and difficult than the silver question, and of far more import to the moral habits and the development of the nation? When leading scholars bring real arguments on both sides of the problem, their work is buried in archives, and no one is moved to action. But when a Chicago minister hangs the American flag over his pulpit, fastens a large patch of black color on it, declares that the patch stands for the liquor evil which smirches the country, denounces wildly the men who spend for whiskey the money which ought to buy medicine for sick children, and then madly tears the black cloth from the stars and stripes and grinds it under his heel — then thousands rush out as excited as if they had heard a convincing argument. And this superficiality is the more repellant because every glimpse below the surface shows an abundance of cant and hypocrisy and search for cheap fame and sensationalism and still more selfish motives mingled with the whole movement; even the agitation itself, with its threats of ruin, borders too often on graft and blackmail and thus helps to debauch the public life.

Those who seriously study, not merely one or another symptom, but the whole situation, can hardly doubt that the demand of true civilization is for temperance and not for abstinence, and that complete prohibition must in the long run work against real temperance. But nothing is more characteristic of the caprice of the masses than the constant neglect of this distinction. Even the smallest dose of alcohol is for them nothing but evil, and triumphantly they seize on isolated statements of physiologists who acknowledge that every dose of alcohol has a certain influence on the brain. This is at once given the turn that every glass of beer or wine " muddles " the brain and is therefore a sin against the freedom of man.

Certainly every glass of beer has an influence on the cells of the brain and on the mind; so has every cup of tea or coffee, every bit of work and every amusement, every printed page and every spoken word. Is it certain that the influence is harmful because an overdose of the same stimulants is surely poisonous? To climb Mount Blanc would overtax my heart: is it therefore inadvisable for me to climb the two flights to my laboratory? Of course, under certain conditions it might be wise to take account of the slightest influences. Without being harmful, they might be unsuited to a certain mental purpose. If I were to take a glass of beer now in the morning, I should certainly be unable to write the next page of this essay with the same ease; the ideas would flow more slowly. But does that indicate that I did wrong in taking last night, after a hard day's fatiguing work, a glass of sherry and a glass of champagne at a merry dinner-party, after which nothing but light conversation and music were planned for the rest of the evening? Of course, alcohol before serious intellectual work disturbs me; but hearing a hurdy-gurdy in the street or thinking of the happy news which a letter has just brought to me, or feeling angry over any incident, disturbs me just as much. It is all the same kind of interference; the brain centers which I used for my intellectual effort are for a while inhibited and thus unfit for the work which I have in hand. When the slight anger has evaporated, when the pleasurable excitement has subsided, when the music is over, I can gather my thoughts again, and it is arbitrary to claim that the short blockade of ideas was dangerous, and that I ought to have avoided the music or the pleasure or the wine.

Of course, if we consider, for instance, the prevention of crime, we ought not to forget that some even of these slight inhibitions may facilitate a rash, vehement deed and check cool deliberation. In times of social excitement, therefore, alcohol ought to be reduced. But again this same effect, as far as the temperate use of alcohol is in question, may result from many other sources of social unrest. The real danger begins everywhere with intemperance: that is, with a lack of that self-discipline which is not learned but lost under the outer force of prohibition.

Psychologically the case stands thus: alcohol has indeed

an inhibitory influence on mind and body. The feeling of excitement, the greater ease of motor impulse, the feeling of strength and joy, the forgetting of sorrow and pain — all are at bottom the result of inhibition; impulses are let free because the checking centers are inhibited. But it is absurd to claim from the start that all this is bad and harmful, as if the word inhibition meant destruction and lasting damage. Harmful it is, bodily and socially, when these changes become exaggerated, when they are projected into such dimensions that vital interests, the care for family and honor and duty are paralyzed; but in the inhibition itself lies no danger. There is not the slightest act of attention which does not involve such inhibition. If I read in my study, the mere attention to my book will inhibit the ticking of the clock in my room and the noise from the street, and no one will call it harmful. As soon as my attention increases, and I read with such passion that I forget my engagements with friends and my duties in my office, I become ridiculous and contemptible. But the fact that the unbalanced attention makes me by its exaggerated inhibition quite unfit for my duties, is no proof that the slight inhibition produced by attentive reading ought to be avoided.

The inhibition by alcohol, too, may have in the right place its very desirable purpose, and no one ought to be terrified by such physiological statements, even if inhibition is called a partial paralysis. Yes, it is partial paralysis, but no education, no art, no politics, no religion, is possible without such partial paralysis. What else are hope and belief and enjoyment and enthusiasm but a re-enforcement of certain mental states, with corresponding inhibition — that is, paralysis — of the opposite ideas? If a moderate use of alcohol can help in this most useful blockade, it is an ally and not an enemy. If wine can overcome and suppress the consciousness of the little miseries and of the drudgery of life, and thus set free and re-enforce the unchecked enthusiasm for the dominant ideas, if wine can make one forget the frictions and pains and give again the feeling of unity and frictionless power — by all means let us use this helper to civilization. It was a well-known philosopher who coupled Christianity and alcohol as the two great means of mankind to set us free from pain. But nature provided mankind with other means of inhibition; sleep is still more radical, and every fatigue works in the same direction; to inhibit means to help and to prepare for action.

And are those who fancy that every brain alteration is an evil really aware how other influences of our civilization hammer on the neurons and injure our mental powers far beyond the effects of a moderate use of alcohol? The vulgar rag-time music, the gambling of the speculators, the sensationalism of the yellow press, the poker playing of the men and the bridge playing of the women, the mysticism and superstition of the new fancy churches, the hysterics of the baseball games, the fascination of murder cases, the noise on the Fourth of July and on the three hundred and sixty-four other days of the year, the wild chase for success; all are poison for the brain and mind. They make the nervous system and the will endlessly more unfit for the duties of the day than a glass of lager beer on a hot summer's evening.

What would result if prohibition should really prohibit, and all the inhibitions which a mild use of beer and wine promise to the brain really be lost? The psychological outcome would be twofold: certain effects of alcohol which serve civilization would be lost; and, on the other hand, harmful substitutions would set in. To begin with: the nation would lose its chief means of recreation after work. We know to-day too well that physical exercise and sport is not real rest for the exhausted brain-cells. The American masses work hard throughout the day. The sharp physical and mental labor, the constant hurry and drudgery produce a state of tension and irritation which demands before the night's sleep some dulling inhibition if a dangerous unrest is not to set in. Alcohol relieves that daily tension most directly.

Perhaps no less important would be the loss on the emotional side, at least for the brain of man. The woman's more responsive psychological constitution does not need such artificial paralysis of the inhibiting centers. The mind of the average woman shows by nature that lower degree of checking power which small alcoholic doses produce in the average man. Without the artificial inhibition of the restraining centers the life of most men becomes a matter of mere business, of practical calculation and prosaic dullness. The æsthetic side of life cannot come to any development because it is suppressed by the practical cares. The truly artistic mind, of course, does not need such artificial help. The finest enjoyment of art, of literature and of music demands a mind in which the suggestion of beauty suppresses by itself all selfish and practical ideas. But the mass of mankind is differently organized. They need some kind of help to open their minds to the message of the unpractical and unselfish. Without such help their instinct would lead them only to trivial and vulgar amusements. Truly the German, the Frenchman, the Italian, who enjoys his glass of light wine and then joyful and elated makes his pilgrimage to the masterpieces of the opera serves humanity better than the New Englander who drinks his icewater and then sits satisfied at the vaudeville show, world-far from real art. Better America inspired than America sober, if soberness is to mean absolute abstaining! In the middle way between this kind of sobriety and intemperance lies that emotional stimulation which for the hard-working masses is an element of true civilization. Can we forget that in almost all parts of the globe even religious life began with cults of such artificial inspiration? For the Hindus the god Indra was in the wine, and for the Greeks Dionysius. It is the optimistic exuberance of life, the emotional inspiration which alcohol has brought into the dullness of human days, and the history of culture shows on every page the high values which have resulted from it.

But with the emotion the will dries up. The American nation would never have achieved its world work if the attitude of resignation had been its national trait. Those pioneers who opened the land and awoke to life its resources were men who longed for excitement, for the intensity of life, for vivid experience. The nation would not be loyal to its tradition if it were not to foster this desire for intense experience. The moderate use of alcohol is both training in such intensified conscious experience and training in the control and discipline of such states. As a child learns to prepare for the work of life by plays and games, so man is schooling himself for the active and effective life by the temperate use of exciting beverages which playlike awake those vivid feelings of success. The scholar and the minister and thousands of other individuals may not need this training, but the millions may best prepare themselves for a national career of effectiveness, if this opportunity is not taken from their lives. History demonstrates this abundantly.

To be sure all this is but half true, because as we said the individual and finally the nation may find substitutes, may satisfy the craving for emotional excitement, for will elation, for intense experience by other means. Gambling and betting, mysticism and superstition, recklessness and adventurousness, sexual over-indulgence and perversion, brutality and crime, divorce and vulgar amusements, have always been the psychological means of overcoming the emptiness and monotony of an unstimulated life. Like alcohol they produce that partial paralysis and create intense experiences. As long as the social mind is not entirely dried up, they take hold of the masses with the necessity of a psychological law.

Has not history experimented sufficiently? Prohibitionist stump speakers may tell us that their cause means the hitherto unheard-of progress of civilization; the United States, after abolishing slavery for mankind, is called on to end also the tyranny of alcohol under which humanity has suffered for ages. But are there not two hundred millions of Moslems who are obedient to Mohammed's law, that wine drinking is sinful? What is the outcome? Of course, it is not inspiring to hear the boast of the Moslems that the Christians bring whiskey to Africa and bestialize the natives, while the Mohammedans fight alcohol. But aside from this, their life goes on in slavery and polygamy and semi-civilization. All the strong nations, all those whose contributions have been of lasting value to the progress of mankind, have profited from the help of artificial stimulation and intoxicants.

But every strong nation also remained conscious of the dangers and evils which result from intemperance. On the whole, history shows that intemperance and abstinence alike work against the highest interests of civilization; temperance alone offers the most favorable psychological conditions for the highest cultural achievement. Intemperance mostly precedes the strongest periods in the life of a nation and follows them again as soon as decay has set in. Temperance, that is, sufficient use of intoxicants to secure emotional inspiration and volitional intensity, together with sufficient training in self-discipline to avoid their evils, always introduced the fullest blossoming of national greatness.   Instinctively the American nation as a whole is evidently striving for such temperance, but a hysterical minority has at present succeeded in exaggerating the movement and in transforming it into its caricature, prohibition.   The final result, of course, will be temperance, since the American nation will not ultimately allow itself to become an emasculated nation of dyspeptic ice-water drinkers without inspiration and energy, or permit vulgar amusements, reckless stockgambling, sensationalism, adultery, burglary, and murder to furnish the excitement which the nerves of a healthy nation need.

How temperance can be secured, the experiences of the older nations with a similar psychological type of national mind ought to decide.   First of all, the beverages of strongly alcoholic nature ought to be fought by those of light alcoholic effect.   The whiskey of the laborers must be fought by light healthful beer and perhaps by light American wines.   Further, a systematic education in self-control must set in; the drunkard must not be tolerated under any circumstances.   Above all, the social habits in the sphere of drinking must be entirely reshaped. They belong to a period where the Puritan spirit considered beer and wine as sinful and relegated them to regions hidden from decent eyes.   The American saloon is the most disgusting product of such narrowness; its dangers for politics and law, health and economics, are

alarming.   The saloon must disappear and can be made
to disappear perhaps by higher license taxation and many
other means.   And with it must disappear the bar and
the habit of drinking standing and of mutual treating.
The restaurant alone, with the hotel and the club, is the
fit public place where guests sitting at tables may have
beer and wine with their meals or after meals,— and all
controlled by laws which absolutely forbid the sale of
intoxicants to certain groups of persons, to children, to
inebriates, and so on.   As long as drinking means to the
imagination of a considerable well-meaning minority of
the nation the present-day repulsive life of saloons and
bars, the minority will find it easy to terrorize and to whip
into line the whole country.   But if those relics of a
narrow time disappear and customs grow which spread
the spirit of geniality and friendly social intercourse over
the foaming cup, the spell will be broken.   Instead of
being tyrannized over by short-sighted fanatics on the
one side and corrupt saloon-keepers on the other, the
nation will proceed with the unanimous sympathy of
the best citizens to firm temperance laws which the sound
instinct of the masses will really respect.   Training in
self-control as against recklessness, training in harmless
hilarity and social enjoyment as against mere vulgar excitement and rag-time pleasures, training in respect for
law as against living under hysterical rules which cannot
be executed and which invite blackmail, corruption, and
habitual disregard of laws — these are indeed the most
needed influences on the social mind of the country.

EPILOGUE

SINCE I uttered these opinions in a popular magazine, a whole literature of socalled replies has grown up. There was no lack of vehemence and an abundance of misstatement but I looked in vain for arguments which could change my fundamental opinion.   Let us only see clearly the point at issue.

We all agree that alcoholic intemperance is one of the greatest sources of human misery, being the direct cause of a large part of crime, of poverty, of illness, of insanity, of early death, and in the next generation, of idiocy and depravity.   Without doubt we all further agree that the American saloon is a most atrocious insult to decent social life and that its influence toward corrupt politics and toward intemperate habits is detestable.   We all further agree that all alcoholic beverages are dangerous for children and psychopathics; and we agree that to fight against such evils is the duty of every conscientious reformer.

Thus our possible disagreement appears only when we consider the means by which these evils can be removed in the highest possible degree without introducing other evils equally calamitous.   After studying this problem for more than twenty years, after repeating frequently in the psychological laboratory all the significant experiments and after curing scores of drunkards by psychotherapeutic means, thus being near to the question all the time, I am fully convinced that under the present conditions of

American life the only wise way of reform is by working toward temperance and not toward prohibition. It must be a campaign of education toward a moderate use of light alcoholic beverages.

Of course, I do not deny that the other side has a much simpler remedy. To exclude all alcohol from this country by prohibition laws seems to get rid of the evil at one stroke; it indeed needs much less effort than a true education toward temperance. But the prohibition movement is just like the free silver movement in economics, or like socialism in politics, or like spiritualism in religion, or like Christian Science in medicine, or like pragmatism in philosophy. They all contain a little core of truth, but their truth is old and they become new-fashioned movements only by new sensational formulations which appeal to the unthinking crowd. But just this always secures at first an immediate cheap victory; a superficiality of thinking prevails in the world and can never resist the enthusiasm of fanatics. I have hardly any doubt that this prohibition movement too, will at first overwhelm by its very superficiality the sober efforts for education and reform in this country, just as the vaudeville and the musical comedy have overwhelmed the serious drama, as the cheap magazine has demolished the bookstore, as the yellow press has captured the masses, and as in a hundred other forms the appeal to superficial judgment has been successful. Of course the reaction comes in time, and the cry for prohibition will disappear as the cry for free silver has disappeared; but much would be gained for the true progress of the country if instead of spasmodic zigzag movements all sober enemies of the saloon would advance in a straight line together.   Otherwise the reaction against a victorious prohibition might too easily lead back to intemperance.

Let us not forget that we want to make laws for a nation whose habitual disrespect for the written statutes has proved in past years to be the chief source of its troubles, and further let us not forget that we want to legislate against a physiological desire which belongs to a majority of men.   The absence of this desire in women or in a large number of men whose nervous system is differently organized can easily be misleading.   I personally, for instance, brought up in a temperance household, have had all my life a physiological dislike not only for strong drinks but also for beer.   But in planning for the millions I should feel reckless and irresponsible if I simply generalized my own chance constitution.   I have no word against the socalled restriction of personal liberty; I know no right to personal liberty if it interferes with the common good, but the more must I demand that this common good be determined by careful observation of the real facts.

The kind of abstinence legislation which prevails in certain parts of the country and is evidently near in others is surely not for the common good.   That it destroys industries and makes hundreds of thousands breadless and deprives millions of a harmless, joyful feeling is still the smallest harm which it produces.   Far more important is the disrespect for law which it creates. Prohibition puts a premium on the systematic violation of law and produces a form of corruption which is still worse than the corruption which irradiates from the licensed saloon. Furthermore it re-enforces drinking in its most miserable and dangerous form. The moderate drinker is cut off, while the immoderate drinker is created. It abolishes light wine and beer; and opens wide the way for the worst kind of whiskey. It eliminates all sound supervision and makes minors and inebriates the favorite customers. A clean surface appearance is bought at the price of inner moral and mental destruction.

Worst of all, the masses who feel the instinctive need of an anæsthetic quickly find substitutes. I speak as a psychotherapist whose experiences cover the whole country when I say that the spreading of cocainism and morphinism, of sexual perversions and ruinous habits among the abstainers is alarming. But even on the surface anyone can see to what a degree of dullness on the one side and of vulgarity on the other the masses are led if the means of physiological relief are cut off from a strong, hardworking population. To fight intemperance by prohibition means to substitute one evil for another; a reform by slow education toward a moderate use of light wine or beer, with complete abolition of the present saloon and of the present disgusting habits, is the only way to permanent success in this country, as long as Americans remain Americans.

The discussion is also distorted when overemphasis is

laid on the fact that a very large number of crimes are committed under alcoholic influence. The reader is made to believe that those same persons would be desirable law-abiding citizens, if they remained sober. The real situation is less promising. We simply must acknowledge that a large number of minds offer insufficient resistance to unsound impulse. The fact that those men indulge in alcohol in an intemperate way is only one symptom of the same make-up which leads to misdemeanor and crime. Their intemperance is itself a symptom of their anti-social tendency and in not a few cases the impulse to drink with its resulting coarse pleasure is probably even a substitute for antilegal impulses. Figures easily mislead there. In certain states much has been made for instance of certain statistics concerning the cigarette smoking of school children. It has been found that those boys who smoke are among the worst in the classroom and the campaign literature of the anticigarette party jumps to the conclusion that the bad standing in the class is the result of the narcotic effect of the cigarettes. Here too, the much more natural conclusion is that those boys of the lower order who are unfit to do their duty well and who are anyhow bad in their standing in school on account of careless education without moral supervision are at the same time those who rush into the miserable habit of cigarette smoking.

Of course, there are not a few who are convinced that alcohol is ruinous for everyone, even in moderate quantities; and it has become the fashion to support this belief by the results of scientific investigations. I am convinced that there exists no scientifically sound fact which demonstrates evil effects from a temperate use of alcohol by normal adult men. Every claim on the one side has been disproved by just as important experiments on the other side. Even on physiological ground, everything is uncertain. Dr. Williams, of New York, tells us that alcohol is never a food; and Dr. Dana, of New York, the president of the New York Academy of Medicine, tells us that alcohol is always a food. Dr. Williams writes that alcohol always lessens the power of work; and Dr. Dana writes that, as proved by recent experiments, alcohol has no effect, one way or the other, on the capacity to work if given in moderate daily doses. Dr. Williams writes that alcohol is the greatest evil of modern society; and Dr. Dana writes that the immediate removal of alcohol from social life would lead to social and racial decadence.

But I, a psychologist, am naturally more interested in the mental side. Dr. Williams and so many others dogmatically assure us, for instance, that alcohol cuts off the power of mental production. But is a psychological laboratory really necessary to demonstrate the hollowness of such general statements? I know scores of men who never produce better than after a moderate use of alcohol, and it is well known that this is true in exceptional cases even where immoderate use is indulged in. I had to hypnotize only recently a well-known New York author whose secret trouble is that he has never written a page of his brilliant books except after intemperate use of whiskey.

Dr. Williams assures us that moderate use of wine and beer reduces the powers of intellectual activity; and again the psychological experiment is said to have proved that. Here I must instinctively think of my teacher who has given to the world the methods of the psychological experiment, the greatest living psychologist. He is seventy-seven years old, has written about forty volumes which are acknowledged the world over as the deepest contributions to psychological thought, wrote last year an epoch-making book; and yet for sixty years has taken beer and wine twice a day with every meal. Two summers ago I attended a number of international congresses and saw there at many banquets the leaders of thought from all nations. I watched the situation carefully but did not discover any abstainers among the sharp and great thinkers of any nation.

To demonstrate that the abstainers enjoy clearer methods of thinking than such drinking scholars would indeed be an interesting experiment, but from the prohibitionist literature I cannot gain the impression that clearness of thinking is their particular strength. Typical of their lack of clearness is the way in which they draw arbitrary consequences from real experiments. For instance, it is quite right to claim that alcohol makes our mental associations slower, but they interpret it as if that involved a destructive crippling of our mental life.

They do not even ask themselves whether or not this retardation of association of ideas may not be a most helpful and useful relaxation of certain brain centers. With the same logic they might demonstrate to us that sleep is a most ruinous invention of nature, as it paralyzes our brain centers still more; and they have not the slightest understanding of the fundamental fact that such an inhibition in certain parts of the brain belongs to every single act of attention. They do not take the trouble to ask whether or not our associations are also changed through the digestion of a dry meal.

With such careless misinterpretations of isolated experiments we could most easily demonstrate that every hour of physical exercise is ruinous for the higher mental life; or that the fatigue from the hearing of one hour's lecture makes mental cripples out of all of us. The fear of those who want to cut off a bottle of light beer from the evening meal of a hard working laborer on account of the psychological experiments is comparable only with the fear of the bacteriophobists. They would like to see every man live isolated in the middle of the ocean because in every other place the laboratory can demonstrate numberless microbes and bacteria.

The only reasonable argument against moderate drinking by normal adult men is a fear that they may transcend wise limits. Yes, in the pamphlets written against my essay I confess the only word which made an impression on me was one contained in a Chicago pamphlet, which said we must consider that Americans are reckless and carry everything to excess. But can that really be the attitude of a civilized nation? To legislate as if the citizens were irresponsible children, incapable of moderation, would mean a degradation of the whole country. With the same justice we might prohibit every sport because it becomes ruinous to the organism if carried to an excess. To be sure the Americans are reckless and excessive; otherwise we should not have ten times more railroad accidents than Europe, and gambling and an absurd chase for money all over the land. But the only sound consequence is that every reformer should educate toward moderation in all fields.

Prohibition removes every temptation. Hence it has no educative influence whatever. To learn to be moderate involves the development of will power which is beneficial in every walk of life. Only cowards who have no trust in their own will prefer to be removed from every temptation. I remember well a man who was president of an abstinence society for many years, and then used for medicinal purposes a glass of brandy. As he had not been trained in any moderation, the one glass stirred up a craving for more until he was lying in the gutter; and when he was brought to me to be hypnotized, he confessed that he had no will to abstain from over-indulgence. The campaign for temperance as against prohibition is a campaign for education which goes far beyond the special purpose, and works against excessiveness and recklessness in every field. If all the enemies of the saloon and of intemperance were to unite on such lines of conservative progress, a real restoration to health and order might soon be secured; the radicalism of prohibition only delays reform until it may be too late.

V

THE INTEMPERANCE OF WOMEN

THE INTEMPERANCE OF WOMEN

IT is a wholesome movement which now turns energetic-
ally against the evils of the American saloon. There
may be disagreement as to the best ways and means, disagreement whether strict prohibition or a real education
toward temperance is the more reliable method but there
is hardly any disagreement as to the fact that the saloon
in its present form with its social, hygienic and political
evils must be wiped out. The day for a widespread reform in the direction of better social habits seems near and
the women claim loudly that thanks for it is due to them.
Their moral sense, they claim, has saved the country.

But may it not be somewhat rash to acknowledge that
the women have a special right to make such a claim, as if
their temperance and their self-control, their moral sense
and their social righteousness had won the victory over
the indecency and intemperance, the selfishness and the
disorderliness of men. They have made no particular
sacrifice in abolishing the saloons where their husbands
and sons and brothers enjoyed themselves, however illusory that enjoyment may have been. They did not have
to carry on a moral struggle in pledging abstinence; they
had never felt attracted by the rum barrel, they never

felt that particular craving for liquor which belongs to the organization of millions of men, but which has only seldom troubled a woman.

Even the firmest believer in the equal rights of women cannot deny that there exist by nature certain bodily differences in the makeup of the sexes and that certain differences of instinct and desire result from it. The longing for that feeling of elation and illusory strength which alcohol furnishes most quickly has at all times and in all nations appeared as a characteristic, or call it a defect, or call it a vice of men. That the women abstain from that for which they do not care is no cause for special moral admiration.

But more than that, in fighting against the saloon the American woman works most directly for her own protection. If the husband spends his money for gin the wife and children are deprived; if he poisons his mind by intemperate use of whiskey the wife will suffer from his irrational vehemence; if he has to pay the consequences of his craving behind prison walls the wife will be without a supporter. The short-sighted man may not see those evils, the weak man may deceive himself, but a woman cannot help seeing and feeling that her own advantage and happiness are at stake. Her cry against the saloon is thus a cry for help; it is a struggle for her own personal comfort and safety; and there is no reason for special praise and admiration for one who enters into a selfish fight against the common enemy.

If the question is raised whether there is a moral merit

in the attitude of women toward this wrong of men we thus have to abstract entirely from the mere denunciation of the saloon and the drunkard. A moral merit which deserves praise would arise only if women were to set a good example, not by abstaining from liquor for which they do not care, but by abstaining from those harmful cravings which arise in female minds and by working with real self-denial for all those aims with which the saloon interferes. If the millions of women were to show heroic abstinence, or at least reasonable temperance, with regard to their own destructive desires, their virtue would show the way for the sinful, stumbling man; but if they are intemperate simply in the lines of their desires their out-cries against the intemperance of the thirsty are at least not imposing.

The women insist, and they are right, that men waste their money in the saloon, and spend thus, for their own selfish enjoyment, that which ought to be saved for the family. Prohibition alone, they say, will prevent the man from throwing away by drink in a night hour what he has earned by his hard day's work. Of course, that is a strictly economic question which must appeal even to the most cruel heart when women tell us that the husband spends for his whiskey what ought to be used on medicine for the sick babies. But are we perfectly sure that it would really have been spent for such a noble cause, for the satisfaction of a serious need or for wise saving in the family's interest — and not, perhaps, for the woman's new hat? Economic questions must be cleanly dealt with from an economic point of view. Can there be any doubt for the neutral onlooker of American society on every social level that man's squandering of money for beverages which he enjoys is still outdone by woman's squandering of money on gowns which she enjoys? And there is only a mild extenuation of this egotism in the altruistic fact that she hopes that he, too, will enjoy her gowns. To say that the millinery stores and the dressmakers profit from the luxury, stands on no higher economic ground than the fact that the drinker gives handsome profit to the bartender and the distiller.

From the higher economic point of view the sums which the feminine members of the American family are spending on their exterior decoration are entirely out of proportion to those which are given for wholesome food, for care of the body, for books and culture, for service and art, for a wise saving or for the public good. No other civilized nation indulges in such waste as this which has become the craving of the fairer half of the nation. It is the one thing which the overfashionable lady of refinement shares with the wife of her tradesman, shares with her most ignorant kitchen girl, and shares with the wife of the most ordinary working-man. The whirlwind changes of fashion are treated like sacred duties.

It may rightly be insisted by the prohibitionists that the pleasure from wine and beer is illusory, as no lasting happiness is attached to it; but is there a more illusory happiness than that of carrying to church the largest ostrich plumes on one's hat? To demand that the hus-

band save his money and overcome his thirst that the
wife may spend it for the satisfaction of her craving vanity
is economically no change for the better.

To be sure, the women will say: " Our fight against
the drinking of men is not only a problem of spending
and saving. Much more important than the mere
economic aspect is the social one. Alcohol ruins the working power of man and thus makes him inefficient; it dulls
his interest and his feeling of responsibility; the drinker
cannot live up to his duties toward his work, toward his
family, toward his community, toward his country. We
want temperance for these reasons higher than mere
money saving." All that is very true, but it suggests
again the counter question: Where is the temperance of
the women in all those functions which destroy the
woman's efficiency and the woman's work for the home
and the country? Where is their self-denial, when their
temptation comes for dulling the mind and for under-
mining their energies? Let us consider the case a little
more closely.

What is, after all, the pernicious effect of an intemperate use of alcohol? Why does the man rush to dangerous
acts, and why is he unable to connect his thoughts carefully and to think of all the consequences, as soon as his
brain is poisoned by whiskey? It means simply this: Alcohol has the power of paralyzing in every brain those
centers which check and regulate the actions of the brain
nerves. The physiologist calls this checking influence
" inhibition," and he would say alcohol prevents the

centers of inhibition from doing their work. In every sober man plenty of impulses come up, but he can inhibit them; if the organism is poisoned by liquor this inhibition fails and the impulse rushes to action. Practically every single disturbance of alcoholic intemperance results from such loss of inhibition. It is as if the supervisor had gone to sleep and all the ideas and impulses do just as they please without control and connection. The craving of man for alcohol results just from the fact that in his sober life these inhibition centers are very strongly at work. They make man efficient for great tasks, but as this represses the freedom of his impulses and the free play of his ideas he sometimes longs to get rid of this supervising master in his mind. Women do not have this longing because their inhibition centers are by nature less active. Woman is therefore somewhat more emotional and less deliberate. Much of the feminine charm results from this weaker development of the inhibitory region in the brain. Woman does not feel it as a disturbance, and therefore has no use for alcohol.

But to be efficient in life, to do our work with energy and to do it well, much more, of course, is needed than mere supervision and regulation. We need, above all, attention and effort; we must be excited from brain centers which furnish the strength and the energy for our thoughts and acts. If those attention centers were not at work our impulses would become flabby, our thoughts would be constantly shifting, our ideas would remain superficial, we should lack the power to hold anything steadily before our minds and to overcome resistance and to live up to our duty. These attention centers are the real well of our higher life, they give to our personality its true meaning and character. No brain destruction could be worse than the paralysis of those centers.

And yet just here sets in the craving of the woman, and with a thousand devices she tries to subdue and to render ineffective these attention centers which trouble her as much as the inhibition centers trouble her husband. There are many ways to render these attention centers inactive. For instance, they can very easily be dulled and benumbed and almost put to sleep by a continuous repetition of monotonous faint impressions, a kind of hypnotizing of the attention. Or it can be done by constantly rushing from one thing to another, each just making a fugitive impression on the mind which is not connected by a firm act of attention with that which went before and with that which is to follow. Instead of expressing it in such terms of physiological psychology let me state it practically by some illustrations.

If, for instance, a man came to my office and complained that he had such a strong feeling of reserve, duty and discipline that he would like to get rid of all these inhibitions quickly, I should give him as a prescription: " My dear man, go into the next saloon and drink a whole bottle of whiskey and all that discipline and order and sense of duty will quickly be abolished."

If, on the other hand, his wife came to my office and should complain that, whatever she undertakes, she puts her serious attention into it, and makes an energetic effort to do it as well as she can, and strives with her whole personality toward high ideals which demand her full power of mind, then I should say: " My dear woman, of course we must abolish such a lamentable state, and I shall give you my prescription. Please begin at first by always sitting in a rocking-chair, which by its monotonous movement has a very nice hypnotizing influence. Take care also that you have a box of candy always at hand; this constant nibbling will aid splendidly in the dulling of your attention. If you do not feel too elegant for it I can also recommend chewing-gum. Then be careful with your reading. You must never read a book where one chapter demands that you hold before your mind what you have read in the foregoing chapter. The right thing for you is to take a half a dozen illustrated magazines at a time and to glance over the pictures; you may read somewhat more carefully the advertisements, here and there you might peep into an article, but take care that there is no inner coherence in what you are reading. It is hardly necessary to advise you seriously to avoid any theaters where the plays have a plot in the old-fashioned way. Farces and musical comedies, in which you never know what they are talking about, are exactly the things which you need, if you supplement them from time to time by a few hours in a continuous vaudeville show. As to your social intercourse, you will be reasonable enough to abstain from earnest conversations; but afternoon teas in which you talk with two hundred persons in three-quarters of an hour can be quite helpful to you. Of course, you will not bother yourself with the education of your children, but you may get good fun out of them, especially if you amuse yourself with them in ridiculing their teacher.

"Yet I am afraid that there will still be lots of empty time which ought to be filled in the service of our cure; and I recommend to you, therefore, something which is still better than the 'patent medicines' in which you believe, namely, Bridge. That has already cured the most desperate cases of serious attention. It is well to accompany this by going shopping from time to time without the aim of buying anything in particular, yet finally buying something which you do not need and do not care for. If your purse allows it, by all means use your motor-car much; it is very unsafe to pass through the country in the slow pace which allows an attentive contemplation of Nature, but I am sure your chauffeur will take care that every impression will rush through your mind without leaving any trace. I know some of your friends recommend also whirling through Europe, spending every night in a different hotel. Indeed that is not bad; but you must surely take care that you do not plan more than six days for Italy — one and a half is certainly enough for Rome.

"If you are of more moderate means do not despair! You can have it all without paying for any automobiles. The least expensive and yet most effective road is to devote yourself to public questions without studying them. Decide the problems of the community over your cup of

tea. There is always some nice fad on the way for abolishing arithmetic from the schools or for educating the
Hottentots; and it is so delightful to talk about it all.
Believe me, my dear woman, all this will cure you just
as safely and just as quickly as your husband is cured
from his trouble by his full bottle of whiskey. He will
not be at home much, but, believe me, you will not either;
and he will feel happy in his tipsiness and you will feel
happy in your ' engagements.' "

But is it necessary that I write out such a prescription?
The man has found his way to the saloon by instinct,
and the craving of the woman for the dulling of her attention has been satisfied by instinct, too. And yet no one
seems to understand that temperance is in the one case
quite as necessary as in the other. The alarming effect of
the intemperance in satisfying such a craving is just as ruinous for the community in the one case as in the other.
The personal efficiency is lost by such a pace in a woman's
life, the home is neglected, the moral development of the
children is not cared for, the money is wasted and public
life is damaged — just the same effects as those which the
saloon produces. Yes, public life is damaged, for it is
ruinous indeed for the community if such superficiality
wins the day. On the one side the institutions and crea-
tions of the nation are dragged down by becoming adjusted to such flabby inattention. The literature is
written more and more for readers whose span of attention is ineffective. The American stage becomes one
great national vaudeville. There are more theaters in

New York to-day than in Berlin; but in the German city twenty times more Shakespeare is played than in the Anglo-Saxon. On the other hand, the public questions, as soon as such superficial women mix in in masses, come more and more under the influence of emotional whims; instead of serious study we have hysterical explosions, spasmodic efforts, useless zigzag movements.

Yes, is not even the part which women play in the public movement toward the abolition of the saloon typical of this superficial sort of action? The problem of freeing the community from the evils which result from man's intemperance is with us and cries out for solution. If it were left to experts who would thoroughly study the economic and social, the hygienic and psychological conditions, steady progress could be hoped for. If instead of it an emotional and whimsical treatment is preferred in which the problem is handed over to those who are influenced by mere feeling, the outcome must be one for which the community will pay heavily by turbulent reactions and unforeseen damages. The problem of intemperance, like any other serious problem, cannot be solved by intemperance of emotion. If a true reform is to come, it must be on both sides. The sermon of self-discipline and of self-restraint is needed by women and men alike.

VI

MY FRIENDS, THE SPIRITUALISTS

VI

MY FRIENDS, THE SPIRITUALISTS

IT has been a great surprise to me. When I came to my first séance with Eusapia Palladino, I expected to see that disagreeable Italian peasant woman whom the newspapers had so often described as coarse and ordinary, uneducated and vulgar. Instead, I found a lady who must have been unusually beautiful in youth, with a delicate humor around her eyes, with an expression of sympathy and almost of brilliancy in her face, with a vivacity and cleverness which would have attracted me in any parlor. This impression grew, and it was emphasized by seeing how much she evidently suffered from the efforts of the séances. I am glad that this sympathy is mutual. When she saw me for the first time, I shivered at the thought that some of my sins of skepticism might express themselves on my forehead; her telepathic gift might tell her something of all the bad things which I printed once before about the spiritualists. But my fear of disaster was quickly dispelled. With her inimitable charm she at once pointed to me as the one whom she wished to have at her best side. She is left-handed, and most of the wonderful phenomena occur on her left side. I was to sit at her left with one hand holding her left hand and with the other hand holding her knees under the table while her left foot was resting on my foot. A friend of mine was holding her right hand and controlling her right foot.

I am happy to say this quick touch of sympathy between spiritualistic mediums and me is an old story. I still remember how quickly I became intimate at a reception in Paris with a delightful English lady, who did not know me and whom I did not know, as in the noise of the festivity we were introduced without understanding one another's names. We were so happy that night; and I never have forgotten the shock which dear old Mr. Myers, the venerable head of the psychical researches, received when he suddenly discovered that his famous medium was in such unholy company. I had, and I have, really the best intentions toward them, and I sometimes feel quite ashamed to think what ungrateful things I have uttered about their gifts. To be sure, sometimes they. have treated me badly, too. How unkind, for instance, was Mrs. Holland, whose trance-writings are so carefully reported in the Proceedings of the Society for Psychical Research! She once wrote in her automatic writing, "Hugo — H. M.— Minsterberg — Hugo," but instead of honoring me by the flattering hypothesis that she might have heard my name before, she refused this possibility; it was the spirit of the late Richard Hodgson who had reported my name to her from another world. But in any case, if there is in the spiritualistic heaven more joy over one sinner who repenteth, the spirits must have enjoyed it greatly, when on that stormy night in the

Lincoln Square Arcade, New York City, I sat down holding the knees of Madame Palladino.

Seriously speaking, it was not an easy decision for me to
accept Mr. Hereward Carrington's invitation to take part
in an investigation of Madame Palladino's famous
powers. I had, indeed, refused such urgent requests
through all my psychological career. I have not considered it a part of scientific psychology to examine the
socalled mystical occurrences. Just because I have always
been interested in the abnormal borderland regions of
mind, in hypnotic and hysteric phenomena, I have been
anxious to draw a sharp demarcation line between such
abnormities of mental behavior and the spiritualistic
claims.

When I arrived in this country, the cult of Mrs. Piper
was flourishing, and I was urged from all sides to study
her sensational case. I saw at once that if I began that
inquiry at all, I should have to devote myself to it with
an energy which would absorb all my time and power.
To visit such séances only as a kind of entertainment
under loose conditions would have been without any value
for science. On the other hand, too many experiences
of others warned me against any concentration of efforts
on that problem. The only clean way seemed for me to
stay away from it entirely. Since those early days, hardly
a week has passed by in which I have not been urged to
examine some mystical case. But I have remained loyal
to my program and refused consistently all contact with
the mystical phenomena. I have never hesitated to ex-

plain my standpoint publicly, and I have been more than glad to see how in the last decade this attitude of caution has spread more and more; and especially, that the discussion on psychotherapy has become liberated from the mystical admixtures.

On the other hand, in spiritualistic circles the accusations grew in warmth. The favorite condemnation was that people like me demonstrate by their behavior a " shallow dogmatism " which is no less unworthy than the most superstitious mysticism. It is the duty of a psychologist to examine the totality of mental occurrences, and he has no right to close his eyes on that which seems to transcend our present powers of explanation. I heard this so often and so impressively that I finally yielded. I simply said : " Madame Palladino is your best case. She is the one woman who has convinced some world-famous men. I never was afraid of ghosts; let them come ! "

Of course this change in my action by no means meant a change in a fundamental conviction which contributed much to my previous reluctance. I do not refer to any philosophical or theoretical conviction, but to the practical one that I myself am entirely unfit for such an investigation. There the public is usually under the influence of a curious illusion. Most people think that a scientist is especially adapted to carrying on such an inquiry, and if a great scholar becomes convinced of the genuineness of the performance, the public looks on that as a strong argument. I am inclined to think that scholars are especially poor witnesses in such a case. They are trained through their whole life to breathe in an atmosphere of trust. The scientist who experiments in his laboratory and studies the laws of physics or chemistry or biology has not the slightest reason to be afraid that nature will play tricks or resort to fraud.   And not only is the material which he studies always genuine, but his collaborators in his workshop are as reliable, as far as good-will and honesty are concerned, as he himself.

If there were a professor of science who, working with his students, should have to be afraid of their making practical jokes or playing tricks on him, he would be entirely lost.   If he weighs his chemical substances, he is not accustomed to watch whether one of the boys has a scheme to pull down the lever of the scale.   Such methods may be at home in the custom house, but no sugar trust enters into a theoretical laboratory.   Everything is done in good faith, and there is perhaps no profession which presupposes the good faith of all concerned so instinctively. The lawyer is on the lookout, the physician has to examine whether the hysteric patient is telling him the truth, the business man hardly expects always to hear the whole truth, the politician is skeptical, the journalist does not believe anything; but the scientist lives in the certainty that everyone who enters the temple of science considers truth the highest godhead.   And now he, with his bland *naïveté* and his training in blind confidence, is again and again called to make inquiries which would demand a detective and a prestidigitator.

Moreover, the best scientific work in one field is not

the slightest guarantee for good observation in another field. It is often remarkable to what a degree a man who is a great scholar in one division may be not only ignorant, but uneducated in his attitude, silly in his judgment and foolish in his conclusions in fields which lie outside of his interests. Finally, there must be much of a temperamental factor in inquiries of this kind. It is curious how much temperamental similarity exists among those scholars who have felt attracted to the mysterious field and who have given dignity to it by their famous names. They represent mostly a splendid type of men, but men who from a psychological point of view would have to be labeled as " negatively suggestible." The psychologist knows negative suggestibility very well. He designates by that name those minds which are inclined to prefer just the opposite of what is suggested to them. Positively suggestible persons blindly accept whatever is offered; in the sphere of science they simply follow the herd and repeat what is told by the master; they are entirely under the control of the prevailing opinions. The negatively suggestible persons do just the opposite. They have their prejudices no less, but they have them just in favor of that which is the opposite of the prevailing opinion. If everybody eats meat, they believe in vegetarianism; if everybody calls the doctor, they are sure that healing without drugs is right.

What I saw was Palladino's regulation performances as they have been described a hundred times. I saw them under favorable conditions. Before she entered the room, I had full opportunity to examine in my naive way the setting of the scene. There was the usual partition with the little board cabinet built in. In front of the cabinet were the two black curtains, behind the curtains in the cabinet a light little table, a guitar and some other musical instruments. The chair in which the medium was to sit stood about a foot from the curtains and in front of it the table at which she was to hold her hands, a very light, roughly-made table without outstanding edges. And besides eight chairs and a large scale for taking the medium's weight, there was no other furniture in the room with the exception of a desk at which a young stenographer did her recording work. The circle of the participants was beyond suspicion, men and women who were honestly interested in examining the genuineness of the phenomena. Some of them were able to speak Italian fluently, an ability which contributes to the medium's good humor. We examined the part of the room behind the partition, saw the electric burglar alarm which is attached to the windows in order to exclude the possibility of outside help; we studied the arrangements by which the various intensities of light were produced and we were well supplied with electric flashlights and similar devices for clearing up the mystery.

Mr. Hereward Carrington, who has brought the medium from Naples to New York and who has arranged all the séances, welcomed us and gave us every opportunity to examine carefully whatever we wanted to study. He is at present the most active prophet of Madame Palladino.

His sittings with her in Naples, where he went as a skeptic and returned as an enthusiast, have been described with scientific exactitude in the last November volume of the Proceedings of the Society for Psychical Research in England. They are the most detailed account of all that happens in Madame Palladino's presence. Mr. Carrington has still more recently published a whole volume on the Italian woman, giving the complete history of her remarkable career, and has succeeded in stirring up unusual interest in this country by the discussion of her case in magazines and newspapers. There is no need of saying that most of the occurrences which I have seen, and which so many others have watched since Palladino's " controlling spirit, John," took quarters in New York, might rather easily be understood, if Mr. Carrington himself were in the game. Suspicions of this have been raised from many sides, and the commercial character of the whole enterprise, constantly covered in the newspapers by references to the so called scientific committee, has very naturally strengthened these suspicions. It would have been better to have put that scientific committee at work from the very start instead of postponing its action more and more.

I am glad to say frankly, that I consider Mr. Carrington beyond suspicion. I have no telepathic gifts and do not know what is at the bottom of his mind, but as far as my experience with men goes, I feel sure that he would not consciously aid in any fraud. If he is putting on a mask, it is much more that he gives himself the air of a scientific inquirer, where his real attitude has become that of the faithful believer. When during the performance in the darkened room he begins in his broken Italian to beg John to stretch out his arm behind the curtain, he seems much more in his natural element than when he speaks about physical energies. Nor have I any suspicion of the stenographer, nor do I for a moment admit the idea that anyone climbs in during the performance. Exactly the same performances have been produced by our medium in rooms in which there were no windows at all behind the cabinet. But I may go further. Those clumsy tricks with which the amateur detectives in the Sunday papers have explained the occurrences are to be ruled out too. It is simply absurd to say that she has large hooks in her sleeves with which in the darkened room she pulls the table upward. These good men do not even know that these so called levitations of the table occur in full electric light with every chance to see her arms and sleeves and to move one's hands between the table and her body.

The first act of the performance is indeed essentially filled by phenomena of table lifting in strong, electric light. The reports show that the circle sometimes has to sit an hour or two before the spirits begin their work. It was not so with us. At my first meeting we sat hardly three minutes before the legs of the table on one side began to lift themselves, then on another side, always falling back suddenly after a few seconds, and finally the whole table went into the air while our hands touched it only lightly and her own hands were often entirely removed from its surface. Little interplays were given by mysterious rappings of the table.   Slowly occasional hiccoughs indicated, as we had often read, that she was beginning to enter into a deeper trance, and the table rapped five times, which means that the spirit John demands weaker light.   The room was darkened and only a few seconds later the second act began.   It was still light enough to see the faces of all as white spots in the room, but not light enough to recognize features.   As usual a strong breeze blew suddenly from the cabinet.   I felt it distinctly on my face and one of the two black curtains which were hanging about a foot behind the back of the medium was blown on the table about which we formed our circle.   Throughout this performance in the dark her two hands, as well as her knees and her feet, were held by two reliable members of our circle.   The curtain was put back and very soon the little table in the cabinet behind the curtain was thrown up and fell down on the floor with a loud crash, and one dramatic event followed another.

In the meantime, four raps of the table in the well-known signal code of the spirits kept giving the order that the members of the circle should talk more.   Suddenly the little table began to creep out of the cabinet into the sitting-room, the guitar gave out some tones, and her immediate left-hand and right-hand neighbors were touched sometimes on the arm, sometimes on the back, and sometimes they felt a hand pull their sleeve.   Now the little table began to climb up from the floor and to reach as high as the elbow of one of us, and finally John pressed his hand and arm from the cabinet against the curtain.   I myself had left the circle and stood behind the medium with a hand on the curtain, and distinctly felt how the curtain bulged out with strong energy. I should not have called it the arm of John, but I did feel a sensation as if a mysterious balloon was heavily pressing against the curtain from behind. In short, I have seen with my own eyes and heard with my own ears and felt with my own epidermis the essentials of those phenomena which have converted men like Lombroso and after him so many other scientists. Yet I for one am no nearer to spiritualism than I ever have been. And if some of my spiritualistic friends claim that I ought to have waited until still stronger phenomena appeared, like those which occurred so often in Naples and part of which can be seen in Carrington's report, I venture to contradict. After seeing the milder feats I had not the slightest doubt that the more surprising acts have been observed by the describers. It makes not the slightest difference whether I personally see the hand coming out and ringing a bell and the arms growing out of the shoulder and the head of the medium looking over the curtain with a neck three feet long. I am sure that if I had spent some weeks more I, too, should have experienced these extreme performances which I can so easily imagine from the printed reports. If I had seen them all myself, my stand toward the whole matter would not have been changed, and my opinions are based as much on what others observed as on what I myself found. Yes, I confess that I should be less skeptical if those stronger occurrences did not exist and if nothing hap-

pened but that which arose in my presence. I am afraid
the more convincing in the eyes of the spiritualists my
séances might have been, the less they would have convinced me.

After all, what is the situation? A table is moving without any visible contact. According to the bolder theory,
it happens by the action of a spirit. But more conservative thinkers say that it is simply an unproved theory that
these movements are brought about by the spirits. Other
facts, they say, may make such a theory probable, but the
movements themselves only suggest that a physical energy
is at work there which science does not know as yet, a
supernormal function of the organism. If we ask why
only so few persons have this energy by which tables and
chairs can be made to move through the air without contact, we justly hear that we have no right to prescribe to
nature which substances shall have particular powers.
Have we not discovered quite peculiar energies, for instance, in radium and thorium which no other substances
in the world have? Radium is not the trillionth part of
the earth. Why may it not be that among hundreds of
millions of men just one or another organism has peculiar
powers too? And if we modestly answer that we cannot
understand a kind of physical energy which would work
in such a surprising way, then we are sure to open the whole
flood of eloquence which has so often streamed through the
spiritistic sermons. Did we know of wireless telegraphy
a hundred years ago? Did we know of hypnotism?
Did we know the Roentgen rays? Has not every day

brought us entirely new discoveries? Has not the whole view of the physical world been changed in every century? Have we a right to prescribe that just this kind of energy has no place in the household of physical nature? Ought we not to take a more modest attitude, willing to learn?

We have heard this so often that it has thrown a kind of spell on all of us and we are ready to follow on this path. All right, we say. So far, we have not the slightest idea how an organism can irradiate this kind of energy, but the future may bring us more light. But now our friends the spiritualists to whom we have given our little finger grasp at once for the whole hand and in the next moment they have the entire arm. If such a woman has an energy to move the table, an energy which we do not yet understand and which no physicist has recognized, can not this energy also move the air sufficiently to bulge the curtains and to pick the strings of a guitar, and to touch the shoulder of a neighbor and to make a wind blow out of her forehead? Of course it can. But, add our friends, is it not very arbitrary to stop there? If there is a mysterious power which moves the air, this means that it pushes the molecules and atoms in the universe under the control of the woman's body. Is there any different principle involved, if we frankly admit that one new grouping of the molecules is then just as possible as another? We cannot deny it; and here we are landed where our friends want to bring us. If a hand or an arm appears through the curtain, is it anything else but a special grouping of molecules? Could not that energy group the atoms in such a way that they appear as a new face? Must we not therefore acknowledge that it is simply a more complex case of such unknown energy which shows the materialization of persons of whom the medium is thinking? Those persons may not have independent existence of their own. Perhaps they can materialize only through the thought of the woman who has these mysterious powers. All this is quite justified. If we allow the first step, it may indeed be difficult to say why we should hesitate before the hundredth step in that direction. If we accept the principle, we must accept the consequences. Our surprise at the hands and faces which fly through the air in the darkened room and touch us on the shoulder and kiss us on the cheeks is no wiser than the surprise of an African savage who sees a locomotive or an airship.

All right. But let us at least understand clearly that if we accept this revised universe, then really nothing of value remains in that poor sham edition of the world with which science and scholarship have wasted their efforts so far. If at any moment a third arm can grow out of our shoulders in order to tickle a neighbor, and if a woman can prolong her neck three feet in order to show her face over the curtain, if a head can suddenly become as small as a fist and then bulge out again, then it is simply silly to fill our libraries with that old-fashioned knowledge which so far we have called physics and biology. From the standpoint of natural science we have to begin anew. We must go back to a view of nature which fits well into the ideas of the savages all over the globe, and the effort of mankind to work out a sort of knowledge which is to eliminate the spirit theories of the primitive peoples has been nothing but a colossal blunder. We may be ready to acknowledge that; but can we really be blamed if before this death sentence on the scientific reason is fulfilled our condemned intellect at least makes use of every possible reprieve and of every opportunity to insist on a new trial? Is it really surprising if before we give up hope altogether, we cry out, " Fraud! "

Those who think that fraud is a harsh word and who think that it would be nicer to admit that a table may lift its legs, really ought to keep those enormous consequences in mind. And those who smilingly say, " Of course the hands and faces and the materializations are humbug, but the minor things may be admitted," cannot blame us if we apply their own principle for the whole field and ask at first in all modesty: are we not victims of claptrap and tricks? I know the reply: " Show us the tricks! " But would it really be a proof that there is no trick involved even if I had no hypothesis?

Hundreds of thousands have seen Houdini and have not the slightest idea how he is performing his feats. I acknowledge frankly that when I grasped the curtain behind Madame Palladino's back and suddenly felt there a sort of balloon or bag pressing against my hand I was startled and had no idea how she did it. It reminded me of a similar feeling which I had a depressingly long while ago. I was seven years old. It was in my native town at the yearly fair and I was sitting in the first row in the

tent of a magician. He suddenly took my hat and pulled
a lot of ribbons out of it. I laughed and felt sure that it
was a trick, but just before he was to return my hat, right
before my eyes he pushed his finger through the crown.
I distinctly saw how it pierced through it and I felt sure
that my new hat was ruined. A moment later the hat was
safe in my hands with not the slightest hole in it, and I
have never understood how he did it. My lasting won-
der became less torturing, however, when I heard later
that the apparatus for that trick costs two dollars and
fifty cents. To be sure if it is fraud, an abundance of
ever-changing schemes must be supplied. Every moment
must suggest new tricks, and only a woman with unusual
skill, unusual talent, unusual strength, unusual resourcefulness and unusual ability to deceive and to mislead could
go through these performances undetected for a single
evening. But just such a woman is Madame Palladino.

The first impression of the whole sitting is one of an
atmosphere of trickery. The performance goes on in a
hall which abounds in psychics and clairvoyants and the
room itself suggests the cheapest claptrap. Yet as I said,
I have not the least suspicion of outside help. But now
the performance begins. She had not held her foot on
mine two minutes, and I believed from my touch sensations
that she had not removed it at all, before I discovered
with my hand that she had exchanged her feet. I do not
know how she did it so rapidly without my noticing it.
Furthermore, I was sure that her hand was holding mine,
her fingers lying on the back of my hand. Only in a

natural way from time to time to change the fatiguing position she removed it just for an instant, and if I had not
watched it carefully, I should have entirely disregarded
such a momentary interruption of the tactual sensation.
And yet I found that for her even such a moment was
sufficient to make a quick movement toward her body.
She has a control of her muscle system which is simply
marvelous.   Even if she raps the top of the table with
her knuckles, she can produce sounds of an intensity which
is astonishing, and which indicate a strength of her motor
apparatus that no one would expect in her.   In a corresponding way her senses are evidently hyperæsthetic.   It
seems to me that the sharp reaction movements with which
she responds to any sudden light are not simulated, and I
suppose, therefore, that she has unusual powers of discrimination.   While she apparently hardly watched the
company she observed most carefully every little occurrence, and evidently can always rely on an abnormal sensitiveness of her ears.

On the other hand, if the conditions are of a kind that
even the best senses could not notice a change, she is just as
little able as any normal person to find out a deception.
Then she herself becomes the victim, as if no spirits assisted
her.   To give a typical illustration: When the room was
light and everything depended upon the greatest concentration of our attention on the table in order to prevent
our noticing any tricks which she might perform with the
curtain, she told us repeatedly that nothing could happen
if we broke the chain.   That is, each must touch with his

hands the hands of his two neighbors; as soon as she saw that the chain was interrupted, the phenomena stopped. But when she did not see it, the interruption had not the slightest effect. In agreement with one of my neighbors, we held our hands so that from across the table it looked as if we were touching, while in reality we bent our fingers inward and had several inches distance between our hands. During that period of breaking the chain, the phenomena came plentifully and she herself repeated that they came because the chain was good. But as I said she was always carefully on the lookout. In my first séance when I stood at the curtain, she promised that the hand of John would grasp me through the curtain from the inside of the cabinet, and she made all the preparations which suggested that John was willing. But with her quick side-glance she evidently noticed that I did not stand there as motionless as at first appeared to her. In the almost complete darkness I was slowly moving my leg upward, standing on one foot and moving the other up as high as her shoulder, covering the space between her and the curtain. From the moment of her head movement which I recognized in the faint light, John changed his intentions and I waited in vain for the curtain performance.

I do not in the least wish to suggest that I really know how she is doing all of her tricks. Some facts were to me extremely suspicious. I noticed, for instance, while I was sitting at her side, that every time before a levitation of the table began, she arranged something between her knees under her clothes. It was often only a quick move-

ment as if she were pressing a button, but I never saw the
levitation without such a preparatory action, though the
knees themselves which I held with my hand were kept entirely quiet.   Moreover, frequently she arranged the folds
of her skirt around the legs of the table as if some forceps
were to hold the table leg from below the gown.   Yet I
acknowledge frankly that I saw some movements of the
table in which I could not discover any contact with her
clothes.   But it must not be forgotten that the most characteristic feature of her performances is just the unexpected
variety.   Phenomena occur just in the instant when you do
not expect them and when your attention is turned to
something else.   When you think that the right leg of the
table will rise up, suddenly the left legs are in the air, and
as soon as you have ever seen the whole table going into
the air, you entirely forget that the lifting of two legs only
can just as well be produced by tilting it under the pressure
of the hand.   In short, the many things which you forget,
or to which you do not attend, or which you wrongly expect, or which you mix up, or which you involuntarily
inhibit, or which you supplement by your imagination
play an extremely large part in the whole performance.
We must keep in mind that we have to do with a woman
who has specialized in these very performances for thirty
years.   Always the same silly, freakish, senseless pranks
repeated on thousands of nights before small groups of
more or less superstitious people under conditions of her
own arrangement, conditions entirely different from ordinary life, with poor illumination and with complete free-

dom to do just what she pleases.   Is it surprising that a
certain virtuosity is secured which understands how to adjust the performance in every moment to the special people
and their special mood and to be prepared for every new
emergency?   Nevertheless, not everyone would be able
to learn the trade which is paid at the rate of five hundred
francs an evening.   She is a great artist, and as a vaudeville show she may be at the head of the profession, but I
do not see how she can overcome in any cool observer the
feeling that it is trickery.

If I abstract from my own chance experiences and think
of that large storehouse which Mr. Carrington and his
friends have filled with their careful observations and of
all those wonderful feats which impressed Flammarion
and Lombroso and so many others, my suspicions would,
on the whole, turn in two directions.   In the first place,
she certainly tries to set free one hand or one foot and
with them to produce a number of phenomena.   It is
not by chance that the spirit John, however manifold
and convincing his performances may be, has never succeeded in doing anything which was more than three
feet distant from the body of the medium.   And sec-
ondly, I think that her comfortable black cloth gown with
which she sits in the dark before the black curtain protects
a number of skillful technical devices which she controls
by her muscles.   Now it is true that her observers assure
us constantly that such cannot be the case because her hands
are held, her feet are held and her knees are held.   She
would therefore be unable to work the instrument even

if it were hidden on her body. But that is a very misleading objection. Let us remember how the Oriental women dance. They call it dancing when their feet may be standing quiet on one spot and their hands may be quiet behind their heads. The muscles of the abdomen and of the chest are nevertheless effective and can be just as well regulated to do as exact work as the hands and feet. Moreover, there would be room for a pair of bellows between arm and chest or between the legs, and such bellows in connection with a little tube system could quite well produce most of the phenomena.

The most curious group of her phenomena is that of producing a breeze either under her gown so that the skirt suddenly bulges out or on the curtain so that the curtain flies into the room, or from her hair. It is evident that any slight connection of a rubber or metal tube with a pair of bellows under the arm or under the bodice could produce such effects without any movement of hands or feet. It is in harmony with this view that all the breezes around her occur together with violent contractions of her whole body. Whenever she is preparing an unusual event, she is straining her arms with all her unusual force. She herself and her friends interpret it as a pumping up of spiritual energy. It seems to me more probable that she cannot produce those stronger abdominal muscle effects without contracting at the same time the arms and legs. Even the hiccough with which her deeper trance begins speaks in favor of this, as it is a cramp in the diaphragm which may result from the abdominal action. There is hardly a doubt that she is really exhausted at the end of every séance, and that she is in full perspiration. It certainly is not easy work. Finally, let us not forget that the more surprising phenomena almost never occur at the first séances. Only when Madame Palladino has worked with the same persons repeatedly do the better events arise. There were no heads for me, but I should certainly have worked up to those heads if I had as much time for this as some of my predecessors. She becomes slowly acquainted with the tendencies, suspicions and inclinations of her clients, and those clients in spite of their best will become more and more suggestible. As soon as a few unexplained events have occurred in the first séance, the second is approached with a greater willingness to accept the miraculous, and the attention is more easily diverted, so that some points which at first would have been watched are now disregarded.

It is true Madame Palladino has been asked to undress a few times, and she also generously permitted the ladies of our séances to examine her clothes. The Naples report tells in detail how she went to the outer room with two ladies and took off some of her clothes. Of course, all that means nothing whatever. First, those bellows, of which I have suspicions, might be embedded in such a way that when they are empty of air they would appear to be a mere lining, and even metal tubes might appear to be simply wires at the belt. And moreover, a woman of such wonderful resourcefulness would really not have the slightest difficulty in undressing slowly in such a way that whatever she wanted to hide could be removed or kept hidden on her body itself, so that a few untrained ladies might easily be deceived. It is most wonderful how her charm and humor remove all indiscreet curiosity. To be sure when two ladies of our party at the beginning of the second evening of my séances examined her clothes rather carefully behind the partition, they did not find any bellows, but just this result favors my theory, since after the search, throughout the whole long evening, not the slightest breeze was felt, no bulging, no wind from the hair or below the table. Evidently the apparatus was removed when the undressing began and could not be restored. On the other evening, the wind blew every few minutes.

Of course, I may be on an entirely wrong track and the mechanism may be of quite a different order. But I have not the least sympathy with those who tell me that even though every single one of her acts might be explained by some complex trick, we must after all acknowledge that there is something genuine, because it is so much simpler to settle all by one common explanation through an unknown mystical energy than to invent a complicated theory of tricks for every single feat. This is just that misleading way of arguing for which the world has so often had to pay the penalty. There are too many people who always believe that if there are many cases of which each one is almost proved, their cumulation is a complete proof. As long as each case in itself still allows the slightest possibility of a different interpretation, the whole sum of the cases remains un-convincing. We know how long it was demonstrated that life could develop itself out of unliving substance, because it was so often shown that animals originated in water in which there was almost no chance that germs had entered from without. A thousand such almosts did not help. When really the entrance of germs is absolutely prevented, organisms have never developed.

As long as there is a possibility of explaining every single miraculous event in some way by some kind of trick hypothesis, we need not be afraid that the mere summing up of ten thousand such cases is a demonstration that causal explanation is not in order. I have my doubts whether a complete demonstration of Madame Palladino's methods will ever be possible. She will not work under other conditions than those which she by long training and adjustment has found to be most favorable for her game, and under such conditions an investigation in the highest sense of the word is entirely impossible. More-over, the fact that she is at liberty at any moment to change the program and to bring in always the unex-pected numbers of the show enhances the difficulties.

I have not even sympathy with the efforts to raise the level of the investigation by introducing subtle physical instruments. That gives to the manifestations an unde-served dignity and withdraws the attention from the center of the field. The events are treated as if a really new energy were involved which we should study in the way in which we examine the Becquerel rays. An exact measurement of those movements only shifts the attention away from the woman and her inexhaustible supply of tricks. I was delighted at seeing a little letter scale in the room. It had been used to find out whether by merely holding her hands on each side of the little tray in which the letter is usually placed she would be able to produce a pressure. I felt that that would be a very clean demonstration. I heard that Madame Palladino had really been asked for that demonstration. It was a new task, but with her wonderful quickness she had found her way out. She held her hands on each side of the tray; the scale showed that a mystical pressure was exerted on the top of the tray, and one of the observers with his high scientific carefulness moved his finger around the tray and convinced himself that there was nowhere a contact between the hands and the plate. But the narrator added that he himself had seen that she had a hair tied to her two little fingers and the hair pulled on the lower part of the scale while the little fingers moved downward. No physical instruments can measure such trickery unless we first learn an entirely new adjustment, for which the scientist as such has no schooling. A master detective might do better.

Of course, there will be some who in reply will fall back on their old outcry that all this is dogmatism and that instead of mere theories of explanations they want actual proof. I am afraid I must be still clearer there. I must report what happened at the last meeting which I attended.

One week before Christmas at the midnight hour I sat again at Madame Palladino's favorite left side and a well-known scientist on her right. We had her under strictest supervision. Her left hand grasped my hand, her right hand was held by her right neighbor, her left foot rested on my foot while her right was pressing the foot of her other neighbor. For an hour the regulation performance had gone on. But now we sat in the darkened room in the highest expectancy while Mr. Carrington begged John to touch my arm and then to lift the table in the cabinet behind her; and John really came. He touched me distinctly on my hip and then on my arm and at last he pulled my sleeve at the elbow. I plainly felt the thumb and the fingers. It was most uncanny. And finally, John was to lift the table in the cabinet. We held both her hands, we felt both her feet, and yet the table three feet behind her began to scratch the floor and we expected it to be lifted. But instead, there suddenly came a wild, yelling scream. It was such a scream as I have never heard before in my life, not even in Sarah Bernhardt's most thrilling scenes.

What had happened? Neither the medium nor Mr. Carrington had the slightest idea that a man was lying flat on the floor and had succeeded in slipping noiselessly like a snail below the curtain into the cabinet. I had told him that I expected wires stretched out from her body and he looked out for them. What a surprise when he saw that she had simply freed her foot from her shoe and with an athletic backward movement of the leg was reaching out and fishing with her toes for the guitar and the table in the cabinet! And then lying on the floor he grasped her foot and caught her heel with a firm hand, and she responded with that wild scream which indicated that she knew that at last she was trapped and her glory shattered.

Her achievement was splendid. She had lifted her unshod foot to the height of my arm when she touched me under cover of the curtain, without changing in the least the position of her body. When her foot played thumb and fingers the game was also neat throughout. To be sure, I remember before she was to reach out for the table behind her, she suddenly felt the need of touching my left hand too, and for that purpose she leaned heavily over the table at which we were sitting. She said that she must do it because her spiritual fluid had become too strong and the touch would relieve her. As a matter of course, in leaning forward with the upper half of her body she became able to push her foot further backward and thus to reach the light table, which probably stood a few inches too far away.

After this scream, at least let us not repeat the ridiculous excuse that she sometimes uses tricks when by chance genuine phenomena do not arise, but that she can perform the same acts at other times by mere spiritual powers. No. We had here the perfectly typical performance. Everything occurred in exactly the same style as in previous séances and the conditions of supervision were the best which she allows at all. To put your foot on hers is never allowed, as the poor woman has a nervous

" weakness " in her instep.   Thus the only allowed supervision of her feet is in being sure all the time that her
foot is on yours.   I did indeed feel her shoe all the time.
When the scream occurred and her foot was caught, I
distinctly felt that her shoe was pressing my foot.   A
hook on the right shoe probably pressed down the empty
left shoe.   If her foot had not been caught -that performance would have been the best in the whole séance
and the cabinet mysteries worked in our presence would
never have been under stricter conditions.   Moreover,
this foot performance without any motion of the upper
half of the body evidently presupposes a continued and
perfect training.   Here she was trapped for the first
time in an act which cannot possibly be explained as an
accidental occurrence; such marvellous athletics must be
explained as a regular lifework.   Her greatest wonders
are absolutely nothing but fraud and humbug; this is no
longer a theory but a proven fact.

I have spoken of fraud, and yet I do not want to be
misunderstood.   I do not think it at all necessary, indeed,
I even consider it improbable that Madame Palladino,
in her normal state is fully conscious of this fraud.   I
rather suppose it to be a case of a complex hysteria in
which a splitting of the personality has set in.   We know
to-day that the hysteric double personality has no
mysterious character whatever, that it results from
certain abnormal inhibitions in the brain — pathological
disturbances which are nearly related to the phenomena
of attention, of sleep, of hypnotism, and so on.   Such

a split-off personality may enter into the most complex preparations of trickeries and frauds, may carry them through with a marvelous alertness, and yet as soon as the normal personality awakes, the whole hysteric action is forgotten.   I suppose that a hysteric disease with complex anesthesias is responsible for her whole life history. When as a little girl she saw the chairs and tables moving around her while she was sweeping the room, she probably passed through experiences which she interpreted in the way most natural to her.   What really happened was probably that she violently moved the furniture without perceiving her own movements and without intention. Her lower brain-centers had reached a hysteric independence and from this simple starting-point probably that complex secondary personality developed itself, and I sincerely believe that she is fully convinced of her own mysterious powers.   It is not she who plays the tricks; it is her irresponsible split-off consciousness which focuses on those silly performances.   It is a fraud for which no one is to be blamed as it belongs in the sphere of the hospital.

Our friends have one refuge left.   They tell us that our stubborn will to detect fraud instead of acknowledging mystic powers is a kind of philosophical short-sightedness.   It is an over-estimation, they say, of natural science and the merely physical aspect of the universe.   They denounce it as materialism, if we try to resist their theory of spirit materialization.   But I am afraid their last defense is their weakest.   In this they are right: Materialism is indeed an impossible philosophy. Materialism is nothing but a certain theory of natural sciences, necessary in natural science but entirely unfit for an ultimate view of reality. Such a view can be given only by idealism.

To be sure, some of our friends have a leaning toward a half philosophy which is neither materialism nor idealism, and which is nowadays often labeled pragmatism. There is nothing absolute, nothing eternal, they say, and truth is only that which fits our purposes. But just such pragmatists ought to resist the spiritualistic pseudo-science with all their energies. Their philosophy ought to tell them that there cannot be any help or any hope for our purposes in the conception of a world which is pervaded with happenings which even the official prophet of Madame Palladino calls " preposterous, futile, and lacking in any quality of the smallest ethical, religious or spiritual value."

Millions and millions have to die every year because some parts of their bodies are diseased. They could be helped and could live on if some slight changes in the organisms could be effected, changes which the physician cannot effect because the laws of nature limit the actions of the body. And now we are to believe that in reality the good-will of the spirits is not bound by such a law, that a neck can become three feet long, that a third arm can grow out of the shoulder, in short, that any transformation of the body can be secured. And the smallest part of such radical bodily changes could have saved those millions who had to die.

But I am not a pragmatist. With every fiber of my conviction I stand for idealism in philosophy, as far from materialism as from pragmatism. I believe that our real life is free will, bound by ideal standards which are absolute and eternal. The truth is such an eternal goal. We have to submit to it and not to choose it as the pragmatist fancies. But the obligation which truth forces on our will does not come from without as the materialist imagines; it is given by the structure of our own truth-seeking will. The mere experience of life is not truth. We gain truth only by shaping the life experience in the service of our ideals of reason. Human knowledge has to remold and reshape the material experience until it forms itself in scientific theories in such a way that a world of order and law is constructed. Our own truth-seeking will thus determines beforehand what forms of thought must mold experience in order to give to it the value of truth. Our own reason thus lays down before-hand the real constitution of the only possible world which can be an object of knowledge, and it is not enough that our friends the spiritualists come and simply answer with the famous political words: "What is the constitution among friends?" The constitution of our reason is indeed everything for our possible world experience, and whatever facts may come to us with the claim to be true, the constitution which our logic has established must decide whether they can be accepted or must be remolded until they are acceptable. If we disregard this constitution, then it has no value and no meaning even to discuss the possibility of disregarding it. We should not know whether we understand one another. We should not know whether that which I mean does not mean the opposite to you. We should plunge into mere absurdity. The principle of ultimate truth must be sought in our own logic and reason and no philosophy can be found by watching the psychic of the Lincoln Square Arcade.

VII

THE MARKET AND PSYCHOLOGY

VII

THE MARKET AND PSYCHOLOGY

A LONG time before New York and Chicago were discovered, there lived an alchemist who sold an unfailing prescription for making gold from eggs. He sold it at a high price, on a contract that he was to refund the whole sum in case the prescription was carried through and did not yield the promised result. It is said that he never broke the contract and yet became a very rich man. His prescription was that the gold-seeker should hold a pan over the fire with the yolks of a dozen eggs in it and stir them for half an hour without ever thinking of the word hippopotamus. Many thousands tried, and yet no one succeeded. The fatal word, which perhaps they never had thought of before, now always unfortunately rushed into their minds, and the more they tried to suppress it, the more it was present. That good man was a fair psychologist. He knew something of the laws of the mind, and although he may have been unable to transform eggs into gold, he understood instead how to transform psychology into gold. Psychology has made rapid progress since those times in which the alchemist cornered the market, but our modern commerce and industry so far have profited little from the advance.

Goods are manufactured and distributed, bought and sold; at every stage the human mind is at work, since human minds are the laborers, are the salesmen, are the buyers; and yet no one consults the exact knowledge of the science that deals with the laws and characteristics of the human mind.

How curiously this situation contrasts with our practical application of physical science! We can hardly imagine a state in which we should allow the scholarly physicist to have steam engines and telegraphs in his laboratory rooms and yet make no effort to put these inventions to practical use in the world of industry and commerce. But just that is the situation in the world of mental facts. The laboratories for the study of inner life flourish, experiments are made, inventions are tested, new vistas are opened; but practical life goes on without making use of all these psychological discoveries. It is, indeed, as if the steam engine were confined to the laboratory table, while in the practical world work were still done clumsily by the arms of slaves.

The only fields in which the psychical experiment has been somewhat translated into practical use are those of education .and medicine. The educational expert has slowly begun to understand that the attention and the interest of the school child, his imitations and his play, his memory and his fatigue, deserve careful psychological study. The painstaking studies of the laboratory have shown how the old teacher, in spite of his common sense, too often worked with destructive methods. Whole school plans had to be revised, the mental hygiene of the school-room had to be changed, educational prejudices had to be swept away.

In a similar way psychological knowledge gradually leaked into the medical world also. The power of suggestion, with all its shadings, from slight psychotherapeutic influence to the deepest hypnotic control, is slowly becoming a tool of the physician. The time has come when it is no longer excusable that our medical students should enter professional life without a knowledge of scientific psychology. They do not deserve sympathy if they stand aghast when quacks and mystics are successful where their own attempts at curing have failed. It can be foreseen that reform in this field is near, and it may be admitted that even those healing knights errant have helped to direct the public interest to the overwhelming importance of psychology in medicine. For education and medicine alike the hope seems justified that the laboratory work of the psychologist for the practical needs of men will not be in vain.

We are much farther from this end in the field of law. Certainly the psychologist knows better than any one that he has neither a prescription to remove crime from the world nor an instrument to see to the bottom of the mind of the defendant or to make the witness speak nothing but the truth. Nevertheless, he knows that an abundance of facts has been secured by experimental methods which might be helpful in the prevention of crime, in the sifting of evidence, and in the securing of truthful confession. Every word of the witness depends on his memory, on his power of perception, on his suggestibility, on his emotion; and yet no psychological expert is invited to make use of the psychological achievements in this sphere. But even here there are signs of progress, for interest in the problems involved seems wide awake.

It is strikingly different with the whole field of economic activity. The thousandfold importance of psychological studies to the life of the workshop and the mill, of the store and the household, has not yet attracted public attention. On the whole, commerce and industry seem to take good care of themselves, and seem little in the mood to philosophize or to beg advice of a psychological expert. Here and there they have taken a bit of laboratory knowledge and profited from it, without realizing that such a haphazard plunge into psychology can hardly be sufficient. For instance, no railway or steamship company would employ a man who is to look out for signals until he has been examined for color-blindness. The variations of the color sense in men are typical discoveries of psychological experimentation. But even here the expert knows that the practical tests of to-day represent, on the whole, an earlier stage of knowledge, and do not progress parallel to laboratory study of the varieties of color-blindness. Further, the transportation companies ought not to limit their signal tests to trials of the color sense. It is perhaps no less important that the man on the engine should be tested as to the rapidity of his reactions, or the accuracy of his perceptions, or the quickness of his decisions. For the examination of each of such mental capacities the psychological laboratory can furnish exact methods. Moreover, the transportation companies should have no less interest in studying with psychological experiments the question of what kind of signals may be most appropriate. For instance, psychologists have raised the important query whether it is advisable to have different railroad signals in the daytime from those at night. The safety of the service demands that the correct handling be done automatically, and this will be secured the more easily, the more uniform the outer conditions. Experiment alone can determine the influence of such variations.

Even this small psychological group, the use of signals for transportation companies, is not confined to visible impressions. An abundance of effort is nowadays concentrated on the fog-horn signals of ships, but no one gives any attention to the psychological conditions for discriminating the direction from which a sound comes. In our psychological laboratories widely different experiments have been made concerning the perception of sounds with reference to direction and distance. We know, for instance, that certain illusions constantly enter into this field, and that the conditions of the ear, and even of the ear-shell, may produce important modifications. Yet no one thinks of studying with all the available psychological means the hearing capacities of the ship officer. A difference in the two ears of the captain may be no less disastrous than the inability to discriminate red and green.

Another field in which a slight tendency to consult the modern psychologist has set in is that of advertising. Many hundreds of millions are probably wasted every year on advertisements that are unsuccessful because they do not appeal to the mind of the reader. They may be unfit to draw his attention, or may be unable to impress the essentials on his memory, or, above all, may not succeed in giving the desired suggestion. The reader glances at them without being impressed by the desirable qualities of the offered wares.

The evident need of psychological guidance has affected a certain contact between empirical psychology and business in this field. The professional advertisement writer to-day looks into the psychology of suggestion and attention, of association of ideas and apperception, and profits from the interesting books that cover the theory of advertising. Yet every row of posters on the billboards affords plenty of material for studying sins against the spirit of psychology. Perhaps there sits in life-size the guest at the restaurant table and evidently rejects the wrong bottle, which the waiter is bringing. The advertiser intends to suggest that every passer-by should be filled with disgust for the wrong brand, while the only desirable one is printed in heavy letters above. What really must happen is that the advertised name will associate itself with the imitated inner movement of rejec-

tion, and the rival company alone can profit from the
unpsychological poster.

But, anyhow, the application of general psychology to
the problem of advertising can be only the beginning.
What is needed is the introduction of systematic experiment which will cover the whole ground of display, not
only in pictures and text, but in the shop windows and
the stores. The experiment may refer to the material
itself. Before an advertisement is printed, the arrangement of words, the kind of type, the whole setting of the
content, may be tested experimentally. The electric
chronoscope of the psychological laboratory can easily
show how many thousandths of a second the average
reader needs for reading one or another type, and other
experiments may demonstrate how much is apperceived
during a short exposure, and how much kept in memory,
and what kind of involuntary emotional response and
muscle reaction is started by every kind of arrangement.
The trade journals not seldom show specimens of skillful
and of clumsy schemes of advertising, and yet all this remains dogmatic until experiment has brought out the
subtle points.

But much more important than experimenting with the
concrete material is the experimental study of the principles involved. This is, after all, the strength of the
experimental method in all fields, that the complex facts
of life are transformed into neat, simple schemes in which
everything is left out but the decisive factor. If the

jeweler wants to display his rings and watches in the window in such a way that the effect of the largest possible number will be produced, it is not necessary that we experiment for him with costly timepieces and jewelry. For instance, we may place twenty little squares of paper on one sheet of black cardboard, and on another from sixteen to twenty-four. After short exposures we ask our subjects to decide on which sheet there are more squares. If the squares on both sheets are arranged in the same way the observer will see at a glance that eighteen are less than twenty, or twenty-two more than twenty. But by trying very different combinations and studying the effect of different groupings, we shall soon discover that with certain arrangements the twenty look like only seventeen, or, with better arrangements, like twenty-two or twenty-three. In the same way we may study the effect if we mix squares and circles, or have squares of various sizes, or some of uniform, some of different color. In short, in the most simple form of experiment we can find out the principles that control the impression of the passer-by as to the greater or smaller number he believes himself to see.

The effort to attract the customer begins, of course, not with the storekeeper and the salesman, but with the manufacturer. He, too, must know psychology in order to make his article as persuasive as possible. Since I began to give my attention to the application of psychology to commerce and labor, I have collected a large number of wrappings and packings in which the various industrial establishments sell their goods, and have received plenty of confidential information as to the success or failure of the various labels and pictures. Not a few of them can be tested quite exactly, inasmuch as the article itself remains the same, while the make-up for the retail sale changes. The same quality and kind of toilet soap or chocolate or breakfast food or writing paper that in the one packing remained a dead weight on the store shelves, in another packing found a rapid sale.

Much depends upon the habits and traditions and upon the development of taste among the special group of customers. But I am inclined to think that if the material is analyzed carefully the psychological laboratory can predict beforehand failure or success with a certain safety. As a matter of course, such factors cannot be reduced to a few simple equations. There is no special color combination that is suitable for chocolates and soap and chewing-gum alike, and the same color combination is not even equally fitting for both summer and winter. And still less can the same head of a girl be successfully used to advertise side-combs and patent medicines and ketchup. But this associative factor is equally open to scientific experiment.

Yet, after all, the make-up of the article and its paper cover are less important than the quality and construction of the goods themselves. The manufacturer too easily forgets that his product is to be used for the purposes of human minds, and that a real perfection of his output can never be reached unless the subtlest adjustment to the mental functions is secured. This is true for the most trivial as well as the most refined and complex thing that is to satisfy human interests. To be sure, small effect would be gained if the seller were simply to look over a text-book of psychology. He might easily be misled. The psychologist can show that a square filled with horizontal lines looks tall and one filled with vertical lines looks broad, but woe to the tailoring establishment that should dress its customers in accordance with that psychological prescription. If the tailor were to dress the stout woman who wants to appear tall in costumes with horizontal stripes and the thin one who wants to look plump in a dress with vertical stripes, the effect would be the opposite of that which was desired. It is not that psychology is wrong, but the application of the principle is out of order. We never look at a woman as we look at a square, comparing the height with the breadth. The vertical stripes in the gown force our eyeballs to move upward and downward and reënforce by that our perception of height, while the horizontal stripes simply suggest to us the idea of breadth. Or, to point to a similar misapplication: There was a painter who had learned from the psychologists that we see singly only those things upon which we focus, while everything in the background is seen by the two eyes in a double image. He thought for this reason that he would reach a more natural effect if he drew double lines for the background things in his pictures. The effect was absurd, as his double picture was now seen with each of the two eyes, while in reality we get a double image by developing one in each eye.

Half-baked psychology certainly cannot help us, but the fact that misunderstandings may come up in every corner of psychology is no argument against its proper use. We should not like to eat the meal which a cook might prepare from bits of chemical knowledge gathered from a hand-book of physiology. The well-trained expert must always remain the middleman between science and the needs of practical life. But if special laboratories for applied psychology could examine the market demands with careful study of all the principles involved, the gain for practical life would be certain.

To analyze the case a little more fully, I may point to a product of our factories that is indispensable to our modern life — the typewriting machine. It may serve as an illustration just as well as a hundred other industrial articles, and it has the advantage that the varieties of the machines are popularly well known. Everybody knows that there are machines with or without visible writing, machines with ideal keyboards and machines with universal keyboards, machines with the double keyboard and machines with the single keyboard on which the capital letters demand the pressure of a shift-key to change the position of the carriage. Psychologists nowadays especially in Germany, have started to examine carefully the claims of the various systems, and the results differ greatly from what the man on the street presupposes. Thus we stand before a curious conflict. The manufacturer must shape his article in such a way that it attracts the customer, but while this holds without restriction for questions of external shape and outfit and packing and name, it may interfere with the greatest usefulness of the article and therefore with the real advantage of the buyer.   Yet ultimately the advantage of the men who use the article must be the strongest advertisement, and it may thus be quite possible that it lies more in the interest of the manufacturer to bring to the market a product that pleases less at the first approach and by a surface appearance, but more in the long run.

The visible writing of the typewriter is a case in point. He who is not accustomed to typewriting and wants to begin it will naturally prefer the writing with visible letters.   He thinks of his ordinary handwriting; he knows how essential it is for him to follow the point of his pen with his eyes.   He forgets that in the visible writing the very letter that he is writing is, of course, invisible at that moment, and the touch of the key perfectly produces the complete letter.   The real effect is, therefore, that he sees the letters that he is no longer writing.   The case is thus fundamentally different from that of handwriting. On the other hand, the amount of attention that is given to looking at the visible words is withdrawn from the only field that is essential — the keyboard or the copy. The visible machine may appear more attractive to one who does not know, but may be less effective through starting bad and distracting habits.   Yet again this may have psychological exceptions.   In the case of those individuals who are absolutely visualizers, the visible writing may be a help when they are writing, not from a copy, but on dictation or from their own thoughts. In that case the seeing of the preceding letters would help in the organization of the motor impulses needed for pressing the keys for the next syllable. It would, therefore, demand a careful experimental analysis to determine those persons who would profit and those who would suffer by the visibility of the writing. The instinctive feeling can never decide it.

But this difference of individual disposition plays no less a part with reference to the other qualities of the various types of machines. The double keyboard demands a distribution of attention over a very large field. The psychological laboratory can easily demonstrate that individuals exist whose attention is concentrated and cannot stretch out much beyond the focus, and others whose attention is wide and moves easily. On the other hand, the shift-key is not merely one of the many keys, but demands an entirely different kind of effort, which interrupts the smooth running flow of finger movements. The psychophysical experiment demonstrates how much more slowly and with how much more effort the shift-key movement must be performed. Again, the analysis of the laboratory shows that there are individuals who can easily interrupt their regular movement habits by will impulses of an entirely different kind, but others who lose much of their psychological energy by so sudden a change. For these the breaking in of the shift-key process means an upsetting of the mental adjustment and therefore a great loss in their effectiveness. Accordingly, the machine that is excellent for the one is undesirable for the other, and the market would fare better if all this were not left to chance.

Even as to the keyboard, it seems that psychological principles are involved which demand reference to individual tendencies. For some it is best if the letters that frequently occur together in the language are in near neighborhood on the keyboard; for other minds such an arrangement is the least desirable. These writers mix up the motor impulses that belong to similar and correlated ideas, and they fare better if the intimately associated letters demand a movement in an entirely different direction, with the greatest possible psychological contrast.

There is hardly any instrument on the market for which a similar analysis of the interplay of mental energies could not be carried out. But let us rather turn to another aspect, the work in the factory itself. I feel sure that the time will come when the expert psychologist will become the most helpful agent in this sphere of industrial life. The farmers have tilled the ground for thousands of years without scientific chemistry, but we know how indispensable the aid of the chemist appears to the agriculturist to-day. A new period of farming has begun through the help of the scientific expert. A similar service to labor and industry might be rendered by experimental psychology. It would even be quite conceivable that governments should organize this help in a similar way to that by which they have secured agricultural laboratories for the farms of the country. The Department of Agriculture at Washington has experimental stations all over the land, and not a little of the great harvest is due to their effectiveness. The Department of Commerce and Labor at a future time may establish experimental stations which will bring corresponding help to the mills and factories and even to the artisans everywhere. There is no establishment that produces without making use of human minds and brains. The mill-owner must learn how to use the mental energies of his laborers in the same way that the farmer knows how to use the properties of the soil. And such help is not only to the economic interest of the producer; it would be perhaps still more to the interest of the workingman and his market price.

The first thought might turn to the safety of the laborer, which is indeed dependent upon various psychological conditions. For instance, the mill-owner is not expected to know what mental factors determine the correct perception of distance, and yet it is evident that a laborer is in constant danger if he cannot estimate correctly his distance from a moving machine. He may be able to see correctly with one eye every part of the machine, but if the other eye is somewhat defective, though he himself may not notice it, his plastic interpretation of his impressions will be insufficient. He will constantly be in danger of putting his hands into the buzzing wheels. Only careful consideration of such psychological elements as build up the idea of distance, and exact tests of the workingman's senses, could eliminate such ever-present dangers.

The captain of industry may feel more interested in bringing out the fullest efficiency of his laborer; but, again, as yet nothing indicates that he is willing to put scientific exactitude into the service of this dominant psychological question. An experimental test alone can decide under what conditions the greatest continuity of effective work can be secured and under what mental conditions the individual can do his best. Methods for studying the curve of fatigue in the individual laborer, or the conditions for his most accurate muscle work, and a hundred similar devices, are to-day already at the disposal of the mental workshop; but probably for a long time to come the foreman will be thought to know better than the expert.

Moreover, it is evident that as soon as this contact between the mill and the experimental psychological laboratory has been perfected, new questions will arise corresponding to the special needs of industrial activity. The technical conditions of every industry in the country can easily be imitated in the laboratory with the simplest means. So far we have not the least really scientific investigation of the psychological effect of specializing, of the division of labor, of the influence of changes in the machines, of the complexity of machines, of the effect of temperature, food, light, color, noise, odor, of discipline, reward, imitation, piece work, of repetition, of distribution of attention, of emotion, and hundreds of other mental factors that enter into the workingman's life. It is simply untrue to say that those things regulate themselves. On the contrary, traditions and superficial tendencies, short-sighted economy and indifference, a thousand times establish methods that are to nobody's interest. The employer and the employee alike have to suffer from them.

We may get an idea of the help that could be brought if, for instance, we think of the methods of learning the handling of machines. There are many industrial activities that demand most complicated technique, and yet the learning is left to most haphazard methods. So far, we know practically nothing as to the most profitable methods of learning these industrial activities. But we have only to compare this situation with the excellent work that modern experimental psychology has performed in the fields of handwriting, typewriting, telegraphy, piano-playing, and drawing. In every one of these fields most careful experiments have been carried on for months under the most subtle conditions. With complex instruments the growth and development of the process were analyzed, and the influences that retarded progress and hampered the most efficient learning were disentangled.

Again we may learn from the case of typewriting work. Any one who writes with the forefingers may finally reach a certain rapidity in handling the machine. Yet no one masters it who has not learned it in a systematic way which must ultimately be controlled by the studies of experimental psychologists. Such experimental analyses of the processes in learning to run the typewriter have been carried through with the greatest carefulness, and have demonstrated that the student passes through a number of different stages. He is not only doing the thing more and more quickly: the essential factor lies in the development of habits — habits of manipulation, habits of feeling attitude, habits of attention, habits of association, habits of decisions in overcoming difficulties; and every insight into this formation of mental connections offers guidance for a proficient training. The experiments indicate the psychological conditions for a spurt in effort, for fluctuations in efficiency, for the lasting gain in speed and accuracy, for their relations to the activity of the heart and to motor activities. In short, we now know scientifically the psychological processes by which the greatest possible economy in typewriting can be secured. There is no industrial machine in our factories and mills for which a similar study has been performed; and yet every effort in this direction would increase the effectiveness of the laborer and the profit of the employer.

Our psychological educators nowadays have studied with all the methods of the laboratory the effects of pauses during the school day. We know how certain pauses work as real recreation in which exhausted energies are restituted, but that other kinds of pauses work as disturbing interruptions by which the acquired adjustment to the work is lost. It would need most accurate investigations with the subtlest means of the psychological workshop to determine for each special industry what rhythm of work and what recesses, what rapidity and what method of recreation, would secure the fullest effect. The mere subjective feeling of the workingman himself or the common-sense judgment of the onlooker may be entirely misleading.

Does not every one know how this inner sensation of strength has deceived the workingman in the case of alcohol? His bottle supplies him with an illusory feeling of energy; the careful experiment demonstrates that his effectiveness suffers under the immediate influence of whiskey. The scientific inquiry in every such case must replace the superficial impression. Moreover, a systematic study would not only inquire how the laborer is to learn the most efficient use of the existing machines, but the machines themselves would then be adjusted to the results of the psychological experiment. The experiment would have to determine which muscles could produce the effect that is demanded with the greatest accuracy and speed and perseverance, and the handles and levers and keys would have to be distributed accordingly. Even the builder of the motor-car relies on most superficial, common-sense judgment when he arranges the levers as they seem most practical for quick handling. The psychological laboratory, which would study in thousandths of a second the movements of the chauffeur with the various cars, might find that here also illusions too easily enter. Industry ought to have outgrown the stage of unscientific decisions, and it is inexcusable if physics and chemistry are considered the only sciences that come into question, and experimental psychology is ignored, when every single business, every wheel to be turned and every lever to be moved, are dependent upon the psychical facts of attention and memory, of will and feeling, of perception and judgment.

It would probably be more difficult to help the actual sale of the commercial products by exact scientific methods, except as far as advertisements and display are concerned. And yet it is evident that every man behind the counter and every sales-girl who wants to influence the customer works with psychological agencies. The study of the psychology of attention and suggestion, of association of ideas and of emotion, may systematically assist the commercial transaction. The process certainly has two sides, but if we think of the interest of the salesman only, we might say that he has to hypnotize his victim. He has to play skilfully on the attention of his shopping customer, he must slowly inhibit in her mind the desire for anything that the store cannot offer, he must cleverly fix the emotions on a particular choice, and finally he must implant the conviction that life is not worth living without this particular shirt-waist. How much the stores would profit if every employee should learn the careful avoidance of opposing suggestions! Whether shop-girls in a department store are advised to ask after every sale: " Do you want to take it with you?" or are instructed to ask first: " Do you want to have it sent to your home?" makes no difference to the feeling of the customers. They are un-

conscious sufferers from the suggestion, but for the store
it may mean a difference of thousands for the delivery
service. The newspaper boy at the subway entrance who
simply asks: "Paper, sir?" cannot hope for the success
of his rival who with forceful suggestion asks: "Which
paper?"

The experimental study of the commercial question may
finally bring new clearness into the relations of trade and
law. To give one illustration from many, I may mention
the case of commercial imitation. Every one who studies
the court cases in restraint of trade becomes impressed
with the looseness and vagueness of the legal ideas involved. There seems nowhere a definite standard. In
buying his favorite article the purchaser is sometimes expected to exert the sharpest attention in order not to be
deceived by an imitation. In other cases, the court seems
to consider the purchaser as the most careless, stupid person, who can be tricked by any superficial similarity. The
evidence of the trade witnesses is an entirely unreliable,
arbitrary factor. The so-called ordinary purchaser
changes his mental qualities with every judge, and it seems
impossible to foresee whether a certain label will be construed as an unallowed imitation of the other or as a
similar but independent trademark.

In the interest of psychology applied to commerce and
labor, I have collected in my laboratory a large number of
specimens which show all possible degrees of imitation.
In every case it is evident that the similarity of form or
color or name or packing is used in a conscious way in

order to profit from the reputation of another article
which has won its popularity by quality or by advertisement.   I have a bottle of Moxie among a dozen imitations of similar names in bottles of a similar shape and
with the beverage similar in color to the successfully advertised Moxie.   Tomato ketchups and sardine boxes,
cigarette cases and talcum powders, spearmint gums and
plug tobaccos, glove labels and vaudeville posters, patent
medicines and gelatines, appear in interesting twin and
triplet forms.   The cigarette boxes of Egyptian Deities
are accompanied by the Egyptian Prettiest and the Egyptian Daintiest; Rupena stands at the side of Peruna; and
the Pain Expeller is packed and bottled like the Pain
Killer.

Not a few of the specimens of my imitation museum
have kept the lawyers busy.   Yet all this is evidently at
first a case for the psychologist.   The whole problem belongs to the psychology of recognition.   There would be
no difficulty in producing in the laboratory conditions
under which the mental principles involved could be repeated and brought under exact observation.   Many obstacles would have to be overcome, but certainly the
experiment could determine the degree of difficulty or ease
with which the recognition of a certain impression can be
secured.   As soon as such a scale of the degrees of attention were gained, we could have an objective standard
and could determine whether or not too much attention
was needed to distinguish an imitation from the original.
Then we might find by objective methods whether the

village drug-store or our lack of attention was to blame when we were anxious for a glass of Moxie and the clerk gave us instead the brown bitter fluid from a bottle of Noxie, Hoxie, Non-Tox, Modox, Nox-All, Noxemall, Noxie-Cola, Moxine, or Sod-Ox, all of which stand temptingly in my little museum for applied pschology.

VIII

BOOKS AND BOOKSTORES

VIII

BOOKS AND BOOKSTORES

I HAVE just come home from a delightful trip on the
European Continent, in which there was never any
chance to be homesick for America. America was visible
everywhere! American acquaintances at every inn, and
at every turn of the road, American goods strewn over
every land. From the Ohio cash-register and the Con-
necticut typewriter and the California fruit and the
Massachusetts shoe and the New York chorus-girl, down
to the little devices with the United States stamp, every
American product seems to welcome the traveler on the
other side. There is only one thing he had better pack
into his trunk beforehand if he wants ever to see it: an
American book.

The American book is practically unknown in the
European Continent. I went to the special bookstores of
foreign literature; they had a hundred excuses in store, but
never the books I wanted. I made my pilgrimage to the
large libraries, and could not find such American books as
no village library in America would wish to be without.
I went to scholarly congresses and talked there with hard-
reading men of all nations, and they spoke of the writings
of American scholars as of the Rocky Mountains, which

they certainly accept as existing, and which may be splendid and wonderful, but which they have never had a chance to see in the original. And on expressing my astonishment, I usually received the reply that it is too bothersome to get American books, as the book-trade of the United States seems without order and system: nobody knows where to find what is wanted. I saw it with my own eyes. An important book by a Columbia professor had appeared in New York in March; in the following August, a German bookstore wrote to the English representative of the American house, and ordered the book for a customer. I saw the reply card which laconically announced from London that the book had not yet appeared in print. I was in Berlin when a little paper of mine in a popular New York magazine stirred up some discussion in America; the discussion went over into the German papers, but the magazine did not follow over the ocean. After hunting for it in vain in the bookstores, where the English magazines were heaped up, I was almost surprised to discover at last a forlorn copy on a hotel news-stand, purchasable for about three times the regular price.

It is easy to make light of this failure of the American book abroad: what does it amount to,— we are asked,— if our latest novel is sold at home in hundreds of thousands, and if our magazines reach every village of America? But even if the dollars and cents in the case may be a trifling matter, there is a more important issue involved. The world-influence of the American mind must suffer if the chief messengers of American thought, the books, are hampered on their way, and if the American scholar and poet and essayist and author cannot be heard in every land. The mist of prejudices against the crudeness and materialism of the New World is still thick and heavy; how can it be dispelled, if those who interpret American ideals and express American endeavors are kept in silence outside of the home boundaries? In our times, when the civilized world has become one, and every newspaper of Europe has its long cables about the most trivial American events, it is a wrong to the world-influence of American culture if our writers are banished from the European Continent by our own carelessness.

Of course, it would seem that good translations might overcome the evil. But what a pitiful tale is made by the haphazard selections of the translators! It often seems as if the French, the German, the Italian translators had carefully chosen the least important and least significant products for their interpretative efforts. In German, for instance, it is true that Mark Twain and Bret Harte, and Poe, and, to some extent Emerson, are well known by translations, but beyond that all is chaos; and among American writers of the last years, Andrew Carnegie and Helen Kellar appear most often in the window of the German bookshop. The great tendencies of modern American writing do not show at all in the chance translations of the day.

And yet the gloomy view of our American book-trade which I brought back from my European travels has, after all, a much more serious meaning. The failure abroad may not count for much, but the impressions in Europe brought it more clearly to my mind than before that the American book to a high degree is no less a failure in our own country; here, too, it does not really reach the readers. Of course, the American buys many books, and pushes the latest novel to its third hundred thousand, but no one who watches the selection closely can doubt that haphazard methods determine the demand and supply, and that superficiality and aimlessness prevail; and the guilt for all of it lies in the disorganization of the book-trade. A change somewhat after the European example is needed, and such a change would be not simply a commercial problem, but truly a social reform. That is the reason, and the only reason, why an observer of American social traits asks for a hearing; a serious injury to the people's mind is imminent — that it is an injury also to the publishers' pocket is secondary.

The well-adapted book at home is, after all, the strongest agency for national culture. It is the only reliable remedy for the saloon and its miseries, and it is the only antidote to the benumbing chase for mere wealth and its pseudo pleasures and excitements. The newspaper with its sensationalism cannot stem the longings of the mind, and the chances are great that those who are not in the habit of reading good books will benefit little even from the rich treasures that the magazines put before them. They glance perhaps at the pictures, they rush through a story, they peep into an article,— the have lost the repose needed for that reading which the library at home suggests and sternly demands. Of course, we are near the truth in blaming for all this the hurry of our up-to-date life. To rush through the world in automobiles means to accustom the eye to the rapid flight of impressions, and spoils the inner eye for the fancies of repose. The woman who wastes her time with bridge whist loses the energy for the old-fashioned habit of continual serious reading. But, however true that may be, is not perhaps the other side equally responsible? Is the book defeated only because the rush of superficial life has become so wild, or has not perhaps the rush become so passionate, and the automobile and the whist so absorbing, because the book was too weak, and did not force itself sufficiently into the foreground?

I point at once to the core of the trouble: in Europe the bookstores are the center of the reading community, and their number increases steadily,— America's bookstores are dying out, and their influence is insignificant; outside of the largest cities you seek them almost in vain. If I go in Germany, for instance, to a town of a hundred thousand inhabitants, I find from a dozen to a score of attractive well-supplied bookstores. A rich assortment of books from all fields — new and older books, literary and scholarly books, popular editions and costly works — is easily accessible to the customer, and by the splendid organization of the trade, every book that is not at hand can be supplied from the central reservoirs in a day. Each store has its ample display in the windows, constantly changing; each one gladly sends to its customers for inspection all the new books which might have special interest for him. The books there come to you and attract you and tempt you and take hold on you.

The average American town of a hundred thousand inhabitants may have a dozen jewelry stores, but not a single true bookstore. Of course there are plenty of chances to buy the stories of the month, and some books on birds and on travel, a golden treasury and a book for the boy; but a full supply in all lines, as it is found next door in the grocery or the cigar or the glove or the ribbon store, is practically unknown outside of the largest cities. The books are sold either in the small stationer's, with ink and leather goods, if not with candy, or in the huge department store, between bathing-suits and trunks. In the one case, there is no backing of capital; all is done with the narrowest means. In the other case, there is no profit, as the books are on the whole added to attract the people who might happen to buy an umbrella and shirt-waist after being drawn into the big place where the latest novel is given away below the publishers' wholesale price. In both cases there is nothing at hand which has not the probability of pretty immediate sale, and in both cases all real interest in literature is absent; an adjustment to the subtler needs of the community is thus impossible.

You might reply: That does not matter, as we Americans order our books directly from the publisher, which saves us the profit of the middleman; the book can be sold so much cheaper because there is no local trade which adds the profit of the dealer to the price. What the publishers have to offer we know sufficiently from their advertisements in the papers, and from their pretty, attractive catalogues, and from the reviews and critical articles. And finally, there are the subscription agents, who certainly lack no patience in bringing their books to the prospective readers. We have therefore stationery shops, and department houses, and publishers' advertisements and selling agents, and in addition the railroad counters and the hotel-stands,— what more can be desired?

All this is granted. But what is the result? Buying books has become to a high degree a matter of passing fashions, and these fashions are essentially determined by the advertisements of the publishers. Everybody buys the latest book which the fashion pushes forward, and the chances are great that it is just that kind of a book which five years later nobody will read, and which will be a dead weight in the home library. No publisher can afford to give equal chance to all his publications. To bring a book, only for a few weeks, to the attention of the magazine or newspaper readers is extremely expensive; it is possible only for the books which, by the name of the author or by sensational features or by special timeliness, promise unusual sale. Any other book, too, might be brought forward by extensive advertising, but it would be ruinous; it may not be difficult to sell a one-dollar book if a two-dollar bill is laid in every copy, but the publishers do not like that method. As a result, most

authors complain that their publishers do not take enough
trouble with the announcement of their particular writings,
and that they therefore sell in unsatisfactory numbers.
They may well envy the German author whose books are
supplied on request to every bookstore in the country
free of charge for a year's display. With us here a
book that is not widely advertised, or widely criticised,
does not indicate its existence to the average reader.
And yet this advertising system itself makes the idea
of reducing the price of books by eliminating the bookstore entirely hopeless; it is more expensive than the profit
of the middleman, and serves only the few favorites.

The immediate consequence of this whole situation is
the rapid disappearance of the books after their noisy
appearance for a few months. Débutantes in our society
are allowed to dance at least more than one winter before they withdraw; but in the catalogues which pile up
on our breakfast-tables the débutante books of the season
are alone admitted, the output of the foregoing year is
forgotten. A book which does not win favor in the first
weeks seldom has a second chance. But that is a waste
of intellectual labor which no nation can afford. Europeans are often surprised to find how wasteful the
American household of moderate means is: the kitchen
makes use only of the best slices, and does not understand
the art of making the less favored parts appetizing by
dainty cooking, and thus serviceable to the household
welfare. The literary kitchen of the nation is much more
wasteful, without being rich enough to be able to afford

such luxury.   To live ever from new books means in this case simply underfeeding.

This hasty rhythm is all the more ruinous because America does not believe in new editions,— one of the saddest features of American bookmaking.   In Germany, for instance, a book outside of fiction is usually revised by the author when one thousand copies have been sold.   It is thus kept living, in steady contact with the progress of knowledge, and in steady adjustment to criticism; thoroughness demands it.   In the United States I know students' text-books sold up to more than fifty thousand copies in the last twenty years with never a word in them changed.   If the book has once found favor, it goes on, by mere tradition, unchanged, however antiquated its statements may be.   The European publisher in such cases would have demanded from the authors a revision at least every second year.   The reason for the difference is clear.   The European book is printed from type for the purpose of making new editions easy, as the type is destroyed after the printing of a limited number.   The American book, on the other hand, is printed from plates, which allow an unlimited reprinting if the book is successful.   It the plates are once made, it is of course much cheaper to go on with unchanged reprinting than to set up a really new edition.   The publisher too often tempts the author into such superficial usage by contracts which allow increasing royalty with the growing sale, and in this way the financial advantage of both author and publisher has made the custom of new editions unusual.   Yet the best chance to bring an old book to new light is in this way thrown away; in Europe each new edition is circulated and reviewed like a new book. In short, very different factors work together to make American books melt away with the " snows of yesteryear."

The well-advertised books disappear too quickly, and the books which do not justify extensive advertisement have no chance,— but all this is the poor fate of books which have had at least the good fortune to appear. Can there be any doubt that this whole situation works from the outset against the appearance of many other books? Not every book has the desire to be a best seller, not every book is written for large crowds, and yet if it had a chance to reach the inquiring booklovers in every home, and to remain for their perusal in the bookstores, it might slowly find a little audience, and might thus in the long run pay the publisher. But the American publisher knows that there is no long run for the book which is not expensively advertised, or which does not appeal to large circles. He cannot risk, therefore, manufacturing the plates, and the elaborate manuscript remains unprinted. The lack of good bookstores, which are just adapted for selling the slow-moving books, thus inhibits the literary production of the whole country. The young or unknown author is pushed into the newspapers and magazines, while his thoughts perhaps demand the book for adequate expression; or he is forced to keep his product unpublished if his work is unsuited to the popular channels.

Scholarship and academic activity suffer immensely from this unwillingness of the publishers to risk the publication of a modest book; and they are justified in their fears, as, under the American system, publication would indeed mean a loss to them. I feel sure that my first four German books on topics of experimental psychology would not have been published by an American publisher, or only at my own expense. In the last year there appeared in Germany, with its sixty million inhabitants, 28,703 new books; in the United States, with its eighty millions, not more than 8112. In magazines, America is far ahead of Europe; their organization is splendid, they know how to reach the American reader; as they do not need the bookstore, but live from subscriptions and news-stands, the publishers can count on success, and thus no plan need remain unrealized. With books, exactly the opposite; the channels of distribution are clogged because for them the bookstores are indispensable, and their meagerness thus works backwards on the timidity of the publishers.

At the same time the bookbuyers become disorganized too. They no longer have that delightful opportunity to spend half an hour once or twice a week in a well-supplied bookstore, and to enjoy the old friends and the new acquaintances before they are brought home for the family hearth. The reader without a bookstore becomes uncritical; with him to work upon, the silliest book can be brought up to a large edition by clever advertisements, and a smart subscription agent can lead him into any trap. The St. Louis World's Fair published an excellent work in eight volumes as a report of its international scientific congress. This scholarly production was sold at first for twenty, later for twelve dollars, and when the interest seemed exhausted, the remaining two thousand copies were given on a small bid to a little publishing firm which was expected to sell the rest for a still smaller price. But the firm knew where our trade-methods have landed us. They took a cheap book of pictures, and distributed the photographs carelessly through the eight volumes; for instance, they had a picture of a naked woman with a crescent in her hair,— they gave it as an illustration to a scholarly report to the Congress about the moon; and so on. Finally they made a showy binding, and then they sold each set by subscription for one hundred and fifty dollars.

What can be done to bring the haphazard and hysterical methods of bookbuying to desirable conditions, from which publishers, authors, and readers may profit alike? Nothing more ought to be necessary than a fundamental reform of the bookstores. We must have in every town large, beautiful, well-supplied bookstores, conducted with some literary instinct. The German method of bringing this about is not applicable in the United States, as here it would be construed as unallowable restraint of trade. The German law allows restriction which American suspicion of monopolies would not tolerate.

In Germany all publishers form one association, no

member of which has a right to sell directly to the
customer; every copy, therefore, goes through the book-
seller. Yet that alone, if adopted here, would not secure
any great advantage, for it would be very doubtful
whether a small town could have its decent bookstore, as
the large stores in the big cities would evidently be able
to give a high discount, and would thus secure the whole
trade by mail-orders. The bookshop in the small place
would then be lost. The really decisive point is, therefore, that no member of the German publishers' association has a right to give books to a bookstore that sells
below the regular retail price. The customer in a little
country town in Germany can thus get his book from
Berlin or Leipzig only at the same price at which the
store in the neighboring street supplies it, and his neighbor can give him the further advantage of a convenient
display. He trades, therefore, in his own town; and in
this way even the smallest place can provide business for a
solid bookstore which is a center of literary interest.

Such an agreement, which stimulates the book-loving
instinct through every county of the Fatherland, involves
indeed a restraint of trade, and the Supreme Court of
the United States has decided against it. The bookstore
which breaks the price agreement with one publisher,
and undersells its neighbor, cannot by any associative
agreement lose the right to get books from other publishers; yet just on that hinges the German success. But
there are other ways to secure similar results, and one
especially which would be the true American way: a com-

bination without monopoly. In every field of American activity the combinations have raised the level of demand and supply; it is high time that we get for the book-trade that improvement which even the tobacco interests have introduced for the sale of their goods. The dusty little cigar-shops of the past are crowded out by the large stores in which the united tobacco companies sell their goods under their own auspices.

It is by all means the best way. In the department stores literature will never take a dignified place, and the little bookstores, or rather half-bookstores and quarter-bookstores, which prevail to-day cannot ever be the germs for the desired development, because there is no capital behind them. Bookstores which are really to serve the ideal interests of American culture must be attractive, large halls with a rich assortment, and a display with comfort for the reader, and that means an outlay of large capital,— which, indeed, will earn more than in the dingy shops of to-day. Places like the six or eight best and finest bookstores in New York, Boston, Philadelphia and Chicago ought to be several hundred in number, spread over the whole land. Their function would be not less important than that of the public library. And all this is possible at once if the publishers themselves would unite their energies, and together create bookstores in which all products of their publishing houses should be on continuous display. They have the capital, and they would find this method ultimately cheaper than their present catalogue system; it would swell the home libraries; it would bring the quiet and modest books to a dignified sale; it would keep the good books alive longer, and would adjust the sale to the really serious needs of the public: a change which would bring a strengthening of every sound impulse in the community.

Something of this kind must be done, or the book-stores will and must dwindle away entirely, and with them the habit of reading a good personally owned book by the home fireplace,— the habit of reading with continued attention, instead of rushing spasmodically through the little cut-off pieces of the illustrated pamphlets. Otherwise, instead of leisurely wandering through the fields of literature, there will soon be only hasty automobiling through them, with a steady increase of superficiality; and, worst of all, the authors will be more and more forced to adapt themselves to such conditions. American literature will become more and more hasty and occasional, while we are all longing for that great, new, upward movement of American literature for which the time seems ripe and the gods seem willing.

IX

THE WORLD LANGUAGE

IX

THE WORLD LANGUAGE

THE Simplified Spelling Board has every reason to spell Success with a capital. Theodore Roosevelt marches in front of the army, brilliant scholars carry the colors, eminent authors beat the drum, great diction-ary-makers belong to the general staff, and Andrew Carnegie looks after the pay-roll; a triumphant progress is thus certain. And even though a word of comment may yet seem proper for one or another who hates to learn anew, certainly the foreigner, at least, ought to keep silent; and one who, like me, spoke the first English sentence of his life only after having been made a professor in Harvard University, should be the last to venture an opinion.

Yet the Simplified Spelling Board says solemnly: "The Board expects and welcomes criticism; it asks only that the criticisms shall be made after and not before the critic has read the publications of the Board." And if in critical mood you turn to the Board's publications, you find very soon that the foreigner is not by any means so negligible a quantity in the matter of spelling. Take the first Circular which the Board has published; you need not read more than the first paragraph, to perceive that after all we " strangers beyond the seas " are very near to the heart of every simplified speller. The opening of the first proud proclamation reads as follows: " All whose mother-tongue is English believe that, if it is not unfairly handicapped, it will become the dominant and international language of the world. For this destiny it is fitted by its use as the medium of the widest commerce and the most progressive civilization, by its cosmopolitan vocabulary, and by its grammatical simplicity. No other existing speech, and none of the proposed artificial international languages has the same adaptability to such a use. There is, however, a widespread and well-grounded conviction that in its progress toward this goal our language is handicapped by one thing, and only one — its intricate and disordered spelling which makes it a puzzle to the stranger within our gates and a mystery to the stranger beyond the seas. English is easy, adaptable, and capable of many-sided development: its spelling is difficult and cumbersome."

Does not such an introduction of the Board's work give to every well-meaning foreigner the right to look into the matter with his own eyes? As regards that question which the Board first raises i. e., simplifying the task of the foreign student of English, no one in the long honorary list, from Chancellor Andrews to President Woodward, seems to be such a trustworthy authority as any little school-boy in France or Germany or Italy. Is it true that difficulties which the foreigner encounters in acquiring his English are those which our simplifiers are

going to remove? This pretension, at least, I venture to
deny with full conviction. Professor Brander Matthews
and his followers gave out at first three hundred words
which are to be improved. Send them over to the boys
and girls " beyond the seas " who are grinding at their
English grammar to-day, and tell them that the happy
day has come when their despair shall be ended. But
they will shake their heads. They will feel as if you
had told them that their history learning was too heavy
a burden, and that therefore, in future, the teacher would
omit the little anecdotes from the lives of the heroes.
No, for them the spell which needs dispelling is not mis-
spelling.

The fundamental difficulty of English for us foreigners
is, of course, the pronunciation; then comes the abundance
of synonyms, then the many characteristic idioms and,
certainly of minor importance, many tricks of spelling,—
but not the spelling of such words as the famous three
hundred words. Let us not forget that the foreigner —
I do not speak of the hotel waiter — sees the English
words before he hears them; and that makes all the
difference. To him, the words are, for a long while,
the printed letters on the page, and he has thus no other
natural interest than that those words shall suggest as
much as possible of their meaning and their internal
structure in their outer appearance. The more hints and
signs there are to indicate which is which, the more easily
he will find his way in the wilderness. The more
vividly the analogies, not of sound but of grammatical

formation, are felt in the look of the words, the more quickly he will feel familiar among the strangers.

Let us take an illustration referring to a large proportion of the three hundred words destined for mutilation. For the school-boy, who begins with the conjugation, nothing is easier than to learn that the ending " ed " indicates the participle. Nothing, perhaps, gives to the eye of the foreign reader such a feeling of safety. That is now gone; the poor boy will have simply to learn by heart the sixty-two new verbs whose participle goes in future without this " ed "-ification. I hear whole classes reciting sadly, " Exceptions from the rule of ' ed ' are *addrest, affixt, blest, blusht, carest, chapt, clapt, clipt, comprest, confest,* and so forth." And if the grammar copies its information from the Circular of the Spelling Board itself, those poor children will read the list of exceptions in a paragraph which itself contains the participles *spelled, mentioned, handicapped, ignored,* and others which seem to them of the same order. There remains for them no other consolation than the thought that these are just " the exceptions," and that their Latin grammar has somewhat accustomed them to consider exception as the legalized cruelty of grammarians; but that such new punishments for foreign children should be invented in Madison Avenue, New York, would strike them as surprising.

But even if after a few weeks' additional training the new exceptions are memorized in addition to the old ones, is it not still true that the foreigner has lost by this

change his possibility of quick and easy orientation in
the seen sentence,— which alone was his purpose? He
has not in mind a well pronounced sentence which he is
trying to write down. Just the contrary: his pronunciation remains for a long while so incorrect and poor that
any caricature of spelling would be for him sufficiently
phonetic. What he needs is to be able to recognize clearly
the inner relations of the words on the printed page.
That alone can attract the foreigner, and every difficulty
in such a direction makes him shrink from the foreign
idiom. But can we doubt that the alteration of the sixty-
two participles works diametrically again his comfort?
Kist is now to be written like *list, prest* like *rest, discust*
like *disgust*. Even the obscuring words with a double
meaning have been increased: *mist* is now *mist* and *missed;*
past is now *past* and *passed;* and yet nowhere unity:
wisht but not *fisht, winkt* but not *linkt*. You could not
make it worse for the foreigner; whether pleasant for the
English-born, it is not for me to utter an opinion.

The vowels do not fare better than the consonants. Of
course, the English child, who hears the simple sounds of
though and *through* in the nursery and learns much later
how to write them, may be irritated by the complexity.
But the foreign school-boy who sees words of that type
has not the slightest difficulty with them. To learn how
they are pronounced is very easy because they stick in the
imagination just through their curious configuration: no
German or French word looks like them — they are taken
as interesting freaks of language, which are the more im-

pressive on account of their very originality. Just so it
was easy for us, in the geography lesson, to read the word
" Worcester." Such grotesque abnormities are quite
handy for the foreigner. Now he is suddenly to see the
word *tho* written like *who*, and once again he loses a convenient landmark in the printed sentence. But perhaps
he is still more puzzled by *thru*, when he is required to
speak it like *shoe* and *true*. And with the edict of the
Board that *clew* become *clue*, *queue* become *cue*, and *woe*
become *wo*, the helps for the eye are gone. You have
only to write the three words *to*, *two*, and *too* simply *tu*,
in harmony with *thru*, to make the phonetic victory complete. Is this a help to the foreigner who asks nothing
but to see with ease the differences between the words?

I started to speak only as a German, but at this point
I am strongly reminded that I have not only a national-
ity but also a profession; I feel inclined to add a word as
a psychologist. If you want to bring about the understanding of a written or spoken sentence, do not believe
that it is most quickly reached by a straight approach. In
geometry it holds true that a straight line is the shortest
way between two points; in practical psychology it is mostly
not true. The natural language knows that, and always
avoids the simplest means because they are not sufficient
for our mental make-up; the mind needs helps and hints
and side-lights, and the more complex the suggestions, the
easier and firmer the grasp.

The phoneticians habitually make here, in questions of
writing, the same mistake which the inventors of artificial

languages have always made in questions of grammar. The heralds of Esperanto assure us, for example, that it is a defect of such badly manufactured languages as Greek and Latin, or German and English, that the same grammatical relation has usually been expressed in various ways at the same time. For instance, when the substantive is in the plural form, it is a ridiculous waste of human energy, they say, to put the verb in the plural, too. If we say, " the child cries," and " the children cry," we indicate by two different methods that it is in one case one baby, in the other case several. If we change the verb, we may leave the substantive unchanged, or vice versa. The artificial language, of course, interdicts such foul play. Yet, while all this might be true for some improved variety of beings, simple psychological experiments can prove that it does not hold for our particular brand of soul. One stimulus does not work easily enough with us; we need a certain superfluity of suggestion. Otherwise, it would not be so difficult to read proof: we overlook the misprints because the wrong letter does not strike us, since a letter by itself comes to our consciousness only by special effort. Every individual letter is strengthened by its neighbors. In the same way, every grammatical point must be brought out repeatedly, one hint must help another, and if two children cry we must say at least twice, in the substantive and in the verb, that it is not one child. Otherwise, we should need an excessive strain of attention, such as the proof-reader needs for the scrutiny of his text, and reading and listening would become an exhausting labor.

In just this way the written image may tell us much which seems logically superfluous since it brings out elements of the word that cannot be pronounced, and which phonetic spelling seeks to abolish. But just as well might we propose to close one eye in reading, for the reason that the nervous processes in the second open eye and in the corresponding half of the brain are a shameful waste of neuron-activity. Indeed, we can read " just as well " with one eye, and hear with one ear; and yet nature knew better: this luxury is economy. Give us as many optical hints for the discrimination of the words as possible, and the more we apparently waste, the more we save. Simplicity and uniformity are the only, real waste, because they demand from us an amount of attention which is ruinous in its cumulation; they perhaps reduce the expense for printer's ink; but they increase neurasthenia among the millions of newspaper readers.

And, quite by the way, is really nothing to be said for those sybarites who like to indulge in the luxury of superfluous letters for the historical flavor they give the word, even where they are not needed for its easier grasping? Our simplifiers want us to write *good-by;* but when the last *good-bye* has been spoken, will the simpler form still bring to our imagination the suggestion of " God be with you "? And when *fantom* is written like fan, and *prolog* like a king of log, and *subpena* as if it were ashamed of its Latin, and so on, do not most of the overtones disappear? Moreover, even these historical side-lights help toward quick discrimination; anything which stands for difference will help to distinguish, and that alone is the purpose. It may be easier to rush with an automobile through the American cities with their rectangular, parallel streets, one block exactly like another; but it is certainly much easier to know at every moment where we are, in the picturesque, irregular streets of Europe, which show the growth of eventful centuries. If superfluous letters must go, why not, at least, begin where no such historical reminiscences are in the way? It is, for instance, well known that the *g* in *foreign* stands there without any historical justification; but it is just these perversities of spelling that our Spelling Board leaves unsimplified.

Let us return to our Circular. We know its first paragraph appealing to the foreigner. The second paragraph changes the topic entirely; and yet, I am afraid, it is the German again who is most nearly touched by the discussion. I thus feel justified in going on with my quotation of this first pronunciamento. The Circular continues as follows: "Apart from its relation to the foreigner, our intricate and disordered spelling also places a direct burden upon every native user of English. It wastes a large part of the time and effort given to the instruction of our children, keeping them, for example, from one to two years behind the school children of Germany and condemning many of them to alleged illiteracy all their days."

If this is the sign under which the reformers hope to win, I, for one, feel sure that their error turns here into a menace. The spirit of this statement contains a subtle but grave danger for our whole American school work.

The consequences must become the more ruinous from the fact that some of the educational leaders belong to the Board and thus unconsciously add the weight of their authority to these misleading arguments.   But my demurrer must not be misplaced.   I subscribe, of course, with full conviction to the view that the American school children are from one to two years behind the school children of Germany.   I should not hesitate to say even that the difference may be more correctly called two to three years. But I deny absolutely that this has anything to do with the difference in the difficulty of spelling the native tongue. It is sufficient to consider the one fact that every German school child has to learn, not merely one method of writing and reading the German language, but two; he studies the international Latin printing and writing which the Germans share with the English, and at the same time the more difficult and more fatiguing so-called Gothic letters in written and printed form.   The writing, especially, in two alphabets, with the difficult Gothic capitals, enormously multiplies the obstacles in the way of the little school child.   If the Germans used only the Latin letters, the child would be surely half a year ahead of his present place in his other studies.   Is it necessary to point to the further fact that the formation of sentences and the whole style in German is more complex and thus needs much more school training for correct expression?

Even the spelling is in many respects not less bewildering than that of English.   It may be that the American who learns German is less aware of the trickery in spelling,

for the same reasons which make the foreigner content
with the English spelling. The American, too, sees the
German words as soon as he hears them, and welcomes
the optical differences between *dir* and *tier* and *ihr,* or between *er* and *leer* and *mehr,* and so on. But for the German child who speaks the words first and knows their
sounds to be the same, the difficulties of spelling arise in
the school-room. It is therefore utterly arbitrary to suggest that the burden of the American school child is
heavier than that of the German; the double German
script is alone sufficient to put a much heavier weight on
the young German shoulders. And yet those German
children are, in spite of their harder work, one to two
years ahead, as the Board confesses.

The only logical conclusion is that this delay in the educational development of the American school child rests
on quite different grounds. It is not difficult to find them.
The explanation lies in the poorness of the average school
instruction: the lack of thoroughness and mental discipline
and accuracy in every subject. This is not the place to inquire into the deeper causes of this fact. We cannot ask
here how far the insufficient preparation of the school-
teachers is responsible; how far wrong methods of instruction; how far the whole spirit of the country which en-
courages and endorses this superficiality; or how far the
carelessness and indulgence of the parents is to be blamed.
But it is certain that the lack of accuracy in spelling har-
monizes completely with the lack of accuracy and of solid
discipline in every other school subject. The blunders in

spelling are more easily visible, but the " illiteracy " in history, geography, and arithmetic is in no way less frequent.

It is, of course, not inspiring that a doctor-candidate should have written to me last week about " excepting " a position; but spelling is there in no worse case than all the other requisites of education.   Are the Germans, perhaps, quicker at figures, or is the American multiplication table also more difficult than the German?   In highly educated Cambridge are two telegraph offices in the shadow of the University.   For years I have sent from them cablegrams to Germany; every word costs twenty-five cents, and nothing seems simpler than to reckon that four quarters make one dollar and eight quarters two dollars. Employees in those two offices have changed frequently, and yet I can report the exact fact that not only has no employee ever tried to calculate the price without paper and pencil, but that the result has been wrong two times out of three.   The last time, the cablegram had nine words, and the young man calculated on paper that nine times twenty-five make one dollar and eighty-seven cents.

And this inability of the large mass of American school children to do anything accurately goes on throughout the high schools and into the colleges.   It cannot be otherwise.   Where the habit of strict mental discipline is not acquired from the very first, intellectual disorderliness becomes habit.   The students may read much, may be industrious, and may absorb immense quantities, but they do not master anything completely.   Whoever feels an earnest interest in American education ought to give to this lack of carefulness and discipline his most immediate attention; from that point alone can we reform and build up.   There alone is the trouble which makes the American school-boy two years behind the German: — because all careless and inaccurate learning is loose, inefficient, and time-wasting learning.   The child must go scores of times over the same old ground, and the teacher must waste endless energy and time with dreary repetitions, simply because the child has not acquired from the start the ability to give full, concentrated attention to the material of study.   If they had given to spelling and arithmetic only half the attention which they used to give to practical things, for instance to baseball, then the school children would stand well in line with the German children, and no spelling reform would be needed as a new scheme for coddling their lazy attention.

But just because everything depends upon a growing public opinion in favor of stricter intellectual school discipline, I call it a calamity that the Spelling Board takes advantage of the alarming state of the schools to spread the impression that the backwardness of American school children results from the difficulty of correct spelling.   If this fairy tale becomes dogma, then every forward movement of serious educational progress is side-tracked again for a long while.   Then there is no longer any one to blame; our women teachers are then splendidly prepared for their task; our school children are in the most excellent frame of mind for hard study; the parents make the

most ideal efforts to develop in the children the sense of
duty and intellectual responsibility; and the only culprit
is the treacherous dictionary-maker who does not write
blest and *blusht*: in short, all that is in future needed for
the thoroughness of our school children is that it shall be
spelled just *thoroness*.

Seriously, this wide-spread inaccuracy demands the common effort of the whole community, and not the slightest
bit of this strength should be diverted.   Instead of sincere
concentrated effort, there comes one arbitrary scheme after
another to captivate the attention of the public.   For a
while we heard the cry that the whole wrong arose only
because the teachers did not know enough psychology.
The public, justly anxious to improve the defective
schools, rushed at once into the psychological track; the
teachers became overfed with psychological pedagogics.
The public felt proud that something was being done, and
yet, the schools still remained backward.   It could not be
otherwise, because no psychology and no pedagogics can
be a substitute for the first demand — that the teacher
shall know the subject which she is to teach.   And the
chase in the wrong direction, of course, delayed progress
in the right one.   This time it is not the teacher but the
pupil for whom the remedy is advertised.   The pupil
must have a simpler spelling-book; then everything will
be all right, and the two years' difference from the German boy will be got over.   I am afraid it will turn attention again in a misleading direction, and the real evil will
go on.   And yet the children deserve something which is

more valuable for life than three hundred simplified words down to *wisky, wilful, woful,* and *wrapt;* they deserve that the school shall give them a training in accurate methods of learning and thought.

But let us hope that the school children are only brought in for stage effect. This seems the more probable inasmuch as it is not quite easy to see how these three hundred changes can disburden the speller at all. For we hear very soon that, in the opinion of the Board, for most of these words both ways of spelling, the simplified and the cumbersome one, have always been correct. You had always the moral right to put down both *omelet* and *omelette, medieval* and *mediæval, program* and *programme,* and so on. These were the fortunate words which could hardly be misspelled; since, on whichever side you fell, it was right. Thus the new prescription makes it harder, for the boy in future has a choice no longer, but must learn carefully to avoid that form which he finds in most books.

Thus, I say, the children are only a side-issue, and the main point is that only the simplified English has hopes of becoming " the international language." We may return once more to this beautiful dream. Is there, indeed, any prospect that English, reformed or unreformed, may become the language of the world? Of course, even the linguistic Anglomaniacs probably do not anticipate that the fifteen hundred other languages will be abolished, like slavery, and all humanity declared free to use the simplified English. Eastern Asia will probably go on with Chinese, spoken to-day by four hundred millions, and with

Japanese; South America will go on with Spanish; the hundred and twenty millions of Russia may go on with Russian; and even German, French, Italian, and the rest may still resist for a while, till they are classed with the languages of the cuneiform writings as extinct specimens. The only serious question, therefore, can be whether we may expect that the non-English-speaking civilized nations will agree to use English as the medium of international exchange. In that case the Americans would need English only, while the Frenchmen would have to learn both French and English, and so forth.

I am convinced that such a time will never come and that in spite of surface indications the chances for it were never worse; every argument for simplified spelling which comes from these hopes seems to me, therefore, completely illusory. When the Volapük people dreamt their short dream, and now, when the Esperanto phantasts have had their so-called international meetings, they have rested always in one fundamental creed which, they said, had the certainty of an axiom: that the political and economical situation of the civilized world makes it impossible for the living language of one country to become the international idiom of all others. And surely no one can attack the Esperanto movement as far as this self-evident principle is concerned.

Esperanto, to be sure, builds on this foundation an utterly unsafe structure, made up from all kinds of broken and crumbled and unshaped pieces, and calls it the temple of international language. The fact that it is nobody's language is its one true recommendation for becoming everybody's language; even though everybody must feel that such a lifeless, artificial syllable series makes no organic words and sentences. It is not and cannot be a language. Such a linguistic manufacture is at best a mechanical tool like short-hand, which might be useful for a few definite purposes,— especially if the manufacturers should succeed in mixing in their laboratory a word code having less the flavor of one particular group of languages than Esperanto. Esperanto is, of course, essentially a mutilation of Spanish and French, and therefore sympathetic to the members of the French Academy, who recommend it because they feel that its international acceptance would throw aside the rights of Teutonic linguistic instincts.

The real mistake of the Esperanto Utopians is that they do not inquire whether the necessity for one exclusive common language has any real existence. There is, perhaps, one field in which a linguistic uniformity must be desired: that of international law. But this monopoly belongs to French and can hardly be taken away: all the international treaties for a long time have been written in French, and their rendering into another language would open endless and dangerous conflicts of interpretation. There is no other field in which community of language is essential. In the international scientific congresses, which furnish the favorite argument for our reformers, hardly anyone takes part who is not in any case obliged to follow scientific literature in at least the three languages of English, German, and French. In commercial relations, success has always come to him who masters the language of the customer; if a business house wants the trade of South America it is more natural to expect that one of its clerks will learn Spanish than that all Argentine and Brazil will learn Volapük, a task about as interesting as that of acquiring the Cable Code.

There remains, of course, the possibility that we travel; and that we feel it our duty to wander through Italy without condescending to learn Italian and to stroll through Paris without a word of French. Then Esperanto is to be our help and blessing. One of the leaders of the movement says: " All that is necessary is that in future every child in the civilized world shall learn in the primary school, besides his own native language, the vocabulary and grammer of Esperanto; then, finally, we may travel even through Roumania, and if a button comes off our coat, we can go into any shop on the street and ask the salesgirl, in Esperanto, for the button, and she will give, in Esperanto, the price of it." What a glorious perspective! To be sure, there may be Americans who have discovered that even in Roumania a full pocket-book speaks a species of international language which is sufficient to buy any variety of buttons. And some others may think it perhaps a little out of proportion that the country boy in Ohio or Illinois, or in Russia or Spain or Roumania, who may never in his life leave his native land and may never in his life meet at home a foreign guest, should yet have to learn a second language in anticipation of a stranger's losing a button. And if the American boy really wastes more than a year in largely unsuccessful attempts to learn the spelling of his own tongue: will he be delighted with the prospect of learning the intricacies of Esperanto, too, which offers only the one consolation — that you can learn it pretty quickly provided you master well your Latin, French, Italian, and Spanish?

One other thing seems to the Esperantists not quite so familiar as it is to anyone who, like me, daily uses two languages. The real understanding hangs on the pronunciation, and this cannot be learned at will. I am afraid the Esperanto learned in the Nebraska country school might, after all, sound like Chinese to the sales-girl in the Roumanian department store; the pronunciations would be too different. Many of my Harvard students can read German scientific books easily; but if they begin to quote, I have to ask them to translate the text into English; and while most of my colleagues are excellent German scholars, I know very few who pronounce my name correctly. On the other side, of course, the same condition prevails. Moreover, as is natural, an unusual foreign pronunciation is less well understood, the less educated the hearer. I remember that some years ago I spoke in a large American city before an audience of a thousand persons, mostly teachers. I spoke for an hour and a half without notes, and they listened so attentively that I felt quite happy in the thought that I had acquired a sufficient grasp of English to hold such a crowd on a difficult subject. But when I proudly left the hall and took a cab to go to my hotel, the driver absolutely could not understand where I wanted to go; my foreign *R*, in speaking the name of the hotel, did not roll as he was accustomed to hear it. I had to write down the name of the hotel, and he looked with pity on the man who did not know any English. And so I always found it much easier to give addresses to teachers than to give addresses to cabmen; how can Esperanto help us in such a chaos of human labials and gutturals?

But all the blunders of the patent-language inventors cannot justify us in denying that their fundamental creed is right; no living language can become to-day the vehicle of intercourse for the whole civilized world, and it is absurd to look for such a thing. The acceptance of any language, were it English or French or Spanish, German or Dutch, Russian or Japanese, would immediately not only crush the pride of the other nations but would give to the favored people such an enormous advantage in the control of the political world and such immeasurable preference in the world's market that no nation would consent to it before its downfall.

For that reason I said that the chances were never worse; the spirit of strenuous, yet friendly rivalry between the nations in the markets of the world was never more wide-awake, and the feeling of national honor was never purer and nobler. The more the hopes for international arbitration become realized, the more they are eager and ought to be eager to keep clear their own individuality, together with their own rights and duties, their own successes and responsibilities.   Andrew Carnegie's liberality may build a palace in The Hague in which a concert of the most enlightened nations speaks justice through its tribunal.   But Andrew Carnegie has not the power to elevate his Simplified Spelling Board in Madison Avenue to the height of a tribunal far superior to any Hague Court: a tribunal which shall decide that English ought to become the one international language because the English-speaking nations have " the most progressive civilization."   And yet just that is proclaimed in the very second sentence which the Board has spoken to the world.

Everyone probably agrees that mere richness of means and plenty of big things do not make up the progress of the world; the real progress lies in the advancement of knowledge, of morality, of art, of religion, of law, of literature.   If the foreigner's learning of English really meant that he acknowledged the superiority of the English-speaking nations in all these realms, the dream of the Simplifying Board would come quickly to an awakening; national pride would justly put English on the blacklist. We should very soon have similar Boards in Paris and Berlin and so on.   No argument can more retard the spreading of English, or of any other language, than that which insists that its mission is to conquer the world. Might not the Germans say with justice that their progressiveness from the days of Luther to the civic and scientific achievements of the present day, has been inferior to none, and that the language of Goethe and Schiller, of Kant and Bismark, must have the same ambition?

Or is the verdict of the Simplified Spelling Board perhaps only a late punishment for the Germans who some centuries ago ruined the English Spelling? The Board itself reports that the earliest printers in England were not Englishmen; mostly they were Germans or Dutch to whom English was a foreign language. They made, of course, blunders in setting up books in a language which they only half knew. The orginal editions of Elizabethan literature thus became " a marvel of typographic incompetency and of orthographic recklessness." And when the reaction brought an agreement for uniform spelling, it was achieved by the acceptance of the standards set by the printers themselves. All that is certainly very bad. But first, even this does not prove that the Germans are less progressive; since they knew how to print at a time when the Englishmen did not. And further, the Simplified Spelling Board ought to be the last group of men to take vengeance, as without the incompetency and recklessness of those old German printers the whole Board might have nothing to do, and the quarters in Madison Avenue might stand empty.

In truth, there is no hope and there is no need for a real international language, either an artificial or a living one. The times of long ago, when the scholarly men, at least, all spoke and wrote in Latin, cannot come back. There is to-day only one international language necessary and possible; the language of good-will and peace and international friendship with the serious effort to understand the motives of our national neighbors and to respect their efforts. This language of good-will cannot be made less useful by any variety of dialects and pronunciations; one may express it in English, another in German, another in Russian or French or Japanese. Yes, this true international language of good-will must spread more quickly, the more serious our effort to learn the foreign living languages; for the safest way to understand the spirit of another nation is by sharing the enjoyment of her finest literature. What is gained by an international word code which aids congresses and travelers and commercial clerks, if it decreases the number of those who can enjoy the language of Shakspeare and Goethe and Molière and Dante? And it is not only the enjoyment of literature and the internal approach to the soul of a foreign nation, it is the incomparable gain from the study of the languages themselves which broadens our whole personality.

The American boy who learns French or Italian or German up to the point where a real feeling for the language begins, must indeed perceive that his horizon becomes a new one. The German language perhaps appears to him difficult at first; then the moment suddenly comes when he feels that a new manifoldness of inner movements has become living in his mind and has brought undreamt-of satisfactions. It is like the experience of a traveler who has seen public buildings only in the classic column style, and who comes to Europe and beholds consciously for the first time the Gothic churches of France and England and Germany. He cannot stand before the dome of Cologne without feeling that there new energies awake in his mind. Never before has he seen these myriads of arcs and curves and figures, all harmoniously controlled by one great movement, toward the tower which points to heaven. This Gothic style is for him a new language of form, and he is enriched for his lifetime. Wonderful and complex like a Gothic cathedral is the dome of the German language, and yet dominated by that perfect harmony which bends the multitude into most wonderful unity. To deprive the youth of such beauties and to make them believe that it is nobler to demand a monopoly for one's own language is certainly not serving the progress of civilization at home.

But whoever studies German besides his English will find there also, and just in its recent movements, how concerted effort can really improve and develop a language without the arbitrary methods of a Simplification Board. It is true that German spelling also has been reformed in recent years and that some changes have been introduced in the schools. I do not want to praise and I cannot even excuse every one of those German spelling reforms; some of them seem arbitrary and poor. But the essential purpose was to make an end of the confusing doubleness in the spelling of many words. Wherever, in the natural growth of writing, a variety of written forms develops together, the decision of competent men can really help to unify public customs.   As far as the American Board has aimed toward this goal, it has done what the Germans did with much success, and every reasonable man ought to support its efforts.   If it decides for *meter* instead of *metre* and for *labor* instead of *labour,* it crystallizes the real tendencies; and certainly no word of mine is directed against such useful endeavors. But that is not the essential work of the Board.   So far there has never been in the writing of our time an uncertain hovering between *thru* and *through,* between *blest* and *blessed,* etc.   The Board, instead of favoring one of two familiar ways, has closed the only known way and laid out a new one which seemed to it shorter.

More than all, what Germany has achieved with still more success and yet almost without the notice of the foreign world, is the purification of its whole style and expression.   In the first place, the clumsy words of Greek, Latin, and French origin are more and more being abolished; private societies have turned public opinion earnestly to this task, and success is even to-day beyond expectation.   Further, sentences have become more lucid and less involved, the whole diction has become clearer, and the choice of words has become more characteristic. It can be said that the German of the best authors of to-day is absolutely different from the German of twenty years ago; a new style has grown up through the persistent efforts of the nation, without any artificial prescription.   Natural growth, and not mechanical construction, remains the life-condition for every element in languages.

But if the Americans begin to allow a Board to prescribe perfectly unusual methods of spelling for mere simplicity's sake, then there is no reason why a rival Board should not start to forbid certain cumbersome words and phrases, and prescribe a simplified grammar. Yes, as soon as, in spite of the Constitution, such matters can no longer be discussed, but must be *discust,* we cannot be sure that the rival boards may not presently form a word trust which will simply dictate which phrase-mills are to be allowed to run and which are to be closed: all for the higher profit of the world language which will ever remain a phantasm, even if you are obedient and write it simplified, with an F.

THE END